Design

'It is virtually impossible for naval experts to see how all of the military and tactical qualities mentioned could be put into 10,000 tons without sacrificing any vital essential. They carry the formidable armament of ten 8-inch guns in five turrets plus eight 4.7 inch guns; they have cruising ranges equal to the large American heavies; somewhat stronger internal protection and armor almost as strong; much greater lengths; speeds of 32 knots on full loads and yet were designed in 1927! Indications are that the Nipponese admirals have cheated on their actual tonnage (and this applies equally well to the Natis) which might be nearer 11,000 or 11,500 standard tons....The Atagos are without doubt superior to any existing American 10,000 ton 8-inch gun cruiser except perhaps for the Wichita which was built well within the Washington Treaty limits.'

(*The Enemies' Fighting Ships*, by Jay Launer, Sheridan House, 1944, at pages 41-42)

Nachi is shown shortly after completion and addition of deckhouses on either side of the bridge. As completed the tower bridge was rather narrow. The navigation bridge had a significant overhang at the rear sides of the superstructure tower.

In a bid to stave off another costly naval arms race, like the one that had contributed to the First World War, a conference was held in Washington from late 1921 to early 1922, primarily seeking to limit competition among the powers in battleship construction. Although other types of warships were limited in overall tonnage, such as aircraft carriers, the cruiser as a type had no such limitation.

In *Brassey's Naval and Shipping Annual* 1923, Admiral of the Fleet Sir F.C.D. Sturdee, penned an article on the 'Naval Aspects of the Washington Conference'. In his article the victor of the Falklands commented upon the status of cruisers. He noted the treaty provisions that: 1. All combatant surface craft, except airplane carriers *(and capital ships)*, are limited to a unit displacement of 10,000 tons, and are not to carry a gun with a calibre in excess of 8in. 2. No restriction is placed on the total tonnage allowed. At the end of the article Sturdee noted that, 'A limit of the size of the ships and of guns has been adopted, thus further reducing

1

competition.' Sturdee asked the rhetorical question as to whether the conscience of the world's powers had improved sufficiently to honour treaty provisions. The drafters of the Washington Treaty succeeded in stopping a new battleship race but failed to see that in their failure to place an overall cap on cruiser tonnage, that the treaty would generate a new building race in cruisers.

At the end of the First World War there were basically two types of cruisers, the old armoured cruiser and the scout/fleet cruiser. The armoured cruiser was an obsolete design, effectively superseded by the battlecruiser. The scout/fleet cruiser design was a much smaller and lighter gunned vessel designed to act in conjunction with the battle fleet to scout for the presence of the enemy. However, the Royal Navy also had a desperate need for a cruiser designed to protect her worldwide trade routes, since fleet cruisers built during the war were designed specifically to operate with the Grand Fleet in the North Sea, so their range was far too short for effective cruising on the very long British trade routes. Neither the United States nor Japan faced the need for a trade protection cruiser. In 1920 most of the newer cruiser construction among the navies of the world was generally similar. Each navy had small to mid-size cruisers with little or no armour. Main armament calibres had evolved from 4in to 6in but most designs still had a significant percentage of their guns placed in wing positions and had broadsides far less than the total number of guns would suggest.

One exception to this standard was a late-war British design. The *Hawkins* class or the 'Elizabethans' were a class

The *Nachi* was the first of the class to complete and the only one to appear as shown in this photograph taken in December 1928. The 4.7in (120mm) guns to the right are hand-operated without gun shields and there is no extension of the shelter deck from the superstructure to deck edge. *Nachi* received power-operated secondary guns with gun shields and shelter deck extension within months of this photograph. The other three class members were completed with these modifications. Also note the significant overhang of the bridge platform at the rear of the superstructure tower.

of cruisers significantly stronger than the typical fleet cruiser. Armed with 7.5in guns and close to 10,000 tons displacement, the existence of ships of this design was a major reason Great Britain agreed to the 8in gun and 10,000-ton limitation on new cruiser construction. The USN had also looked into the possibility of producing cruisers of similar design but armed with 8in guns and so was also in favour of these arbitrary design constraints. Japan had no fleet cruisers remotely approaching this limit and so she too agreed to these individual ship limitations. All new cruiser designs were initially typed as light cruisers, as opposed to the obsolete armoured cruisers, regardless of whether they mounted 4in, 6in or 8in guns. Cruisers armed with 8in guns were not classified as heavy cruisers until the London Treaty of 1930 subdivided the cruiser category into light and heavy categories based not on displacement but on gun

The bow of *Myoko* in 1933 clearly shows her sheer and flare. The ship is as completed with 7.9in (200mm) main guns, which were not replaced by 8in (203mm) guns until the Second Modernisation in 1939.

size. All cruisers of 6.1in and smaller armament were called light cruisers and those armed with 8in to 6.1in guns were classified as heavy cruisers.

When Japan signed the Washington Treaty in February 1921, her navy already had on the drawing-board a cruiser design that would be her answer to the British 'Elizabethans'. This was the *Furutaka* class, which mounted six 200mm (7.9in) guns in six centreline gun houses. She also had plans for an experimental cruiser designed to employ weight saving measures. With the design for the *Yubari*, side armour was an integral part of the hull, rather than being added over an existing hull as was the traditional practice.

However, in spite of all weight-saving measures adopted by the Imperial Japanese Navy, her warship design process had a consistent and significant flaw. Almost every cruiser design was completed with a displacement far in excess of the design calculations. This trend started with the *Yubari*. Older cruiser designs had come in over calculated weight, such as the *Kuma* class at 1.5% over and *Sendai* class at 5.5% over designed weight but *Yubari* was 14% over designed weight. With the *Furutaka* class, the systemic under-calculation of weight remained in the design process. Although this class added an undulating sheer line as a weight-saving measure, the ships were still 11% over designed weight as completed. On trials the six-gunned *Furutaka* design was run at 9,502 tons and the following *Aoba* design at 9,820 tons. Although neither design exceeded the treaty limit, the incorrect designed displacements of 8,586 tons and 8,910 tons were still the figures reported. The Japanese '2/3 Trial Weight' used different criteria from the Washington Treaty's 'Standard Weight'. The 2/3 trial weight included 2/3rds of the weight of fuel, reserve feed water, and lubricating oil and was measured in metric tons. Standard Weight, measured in English tons, created as the reporting paradigm for the Washington Treaty, did not include the weight of the fuel, lubricating oil or reserve feed water, which added substantially to trial or operational displacement. As an example, the *Aoba* class was to be of 7,500 tons standard and 8,910 tons 2/3 trial displacement. However, an increase of more than 10% over either figure plays havoc with the ship's design.

Cruisers with displacements so far over design weights clearly reflect a major flaw in the design process, although the reasons have never been satisfactorily explained. However, what is clear is that the Japanese Navy made no effort to correct the flaws of the design system. The Imperial Japanese Navy may not have intended to exceed the limitations of the Washington

Treaty to begin with but they clearly wanted to keep their defective system in place. Why would they not correct such a significant failing? Perhaps they thought the errors were aberrations or may be they found the defective design process a useful fig leaf to conceal cruisers that were in fact over the 10,000-ton treaty limit.

The loophole of the Washington Treaty was the lack of a cap on total tonnage in cruiser construction. With no limit on total tonnage, why would any power wish to build inferior cruisers that did not have 8in guns and approach or hit the 10,000-ton ceiling? In this situation the maximum cruiser limitations became the standard cruiser characteristics and almost all new cruiser designs after February 1921 and before the London Treaty of 1930 were 8in gunned, 10,000-ton designs which became known as Treaty cruisers. The Royal Navy stayed with twin 8in turrets with the large 'County' class cruisers, while the USN went with triple gun turrets as a weight-saving measure. The Japanese wanted cruisers that would be superior to the RN 'County' class with their eight 8in guns and the American cruisers with their nine 8in guns (ten guns in *Pensacola* class). That could not be achieved without a design significantly larger in size and displacement than the *Aoba* class.

As can be seen in this photograph of *Myoko* in 1933, the class had very clean lines upon completion. The natural canvas dodgers and main gun blast bags stand out starkly from the dark grey paint scheme. This photograph was one of a number taken at Singapore from USS *Augusta* (CA-31). This was one of the first opportunities for a unit of the class to be viewed by the western navies.

THE *MYOKO* CLASS

In July 1922, after Japan had signed but not ratified the Washington Treaty, a new naval program proposed four new 10,000-ton cruisers, as well as two more 7,500-ton cruisers, which was the *Aoba* class. Authorised in March 1923 the new 10,000-ton design was known officially as *large model cruisers*. The

original requirement was for eight 200mm guns in three twin mounts forward and one twin mount aft, four 120mm (4.7in) guns, eight 610mm torpedo tubes in four twin fixed mountings, protection against 200mm shells in indirect fire and 6in shells for flat trajectory direct fire for critical areas, a 10,000 nautical mile range at 13.5 knots, and a maximum speed of 35.5 knots. Captain Hiraga Yuzuru was assigned as Constructor for the design. Captain Hiraga convinced the naval staff to make some changes to the requirements. These were an increase in main armament to ten 200mm guns, reduction of range to 8,000nm at 13.5 knots and deletion of torpedo armament. Captain Hiraga thought the torpedo mounts, located inside the hull above the engine spaces, would present as much danger to the ships themselves as to the enemy. Hiraga was promoted

to Rear Admiral and Lieutenant Commander Fujimoto Kikuo took over the design. The design was approved on 23 August 1923. The new cruisers were to be 10,000 tons standard in English tons, 11,850 metric tons at 2/3 trial displacement, so the original construction order had the ships meeting the terms of the Washington Treaty.

However, additions were quickly made to the design, each of which added weight. The Torpedo Branch convinced the Naval General Staff to add back the four twin tube torpedo armament and the staff increased the secondary to six 120mm HA single gun mounts. While the ships were under construction the twin tubes were changed to triple tubes and in 1928 a deckhouse on either side of the bridge and forward stack was added for additional living accommodation. The Naval General Staff calculated that these changes would add 500 metric tons and that the revised 2/3 trial displacement would be 12,350 metric tons. Since the original design was right at the treaty limit, the staff knowingly exceeded treaty limitations with these additions. Called the *Myoko* class, the first of the cruisers to complete was *Nachi*. The trial displacement of *Nachi* was 13,338 metric tons, which was 12% over design trial displacement. This would place the ship at about 11,250 tons standard, clearly in violation of treaty limits. Of course the Japanese reported the design as in compliance with the treaty.

As built the *Myoko* class had an armour belt of 102mm in thickness and inclined inward at 12 degrees. The belt started forward of No 1 barbette and ended aft of No 5 barbette. For torpedo and mine protection, the ship was fitted with underwater bulges that were 300 feet (93m) long and 8 feet (2.5m) in

The amidships superstructure presents an impressive profile. Notice the extensive use of natural canvas dodgers. This photograph reflects the appearance of the cruisers of the *Myoko* class as completed with six 4.7in (120mm).

Myoko Class as designed 1924	
Dimensions	Length oa 668.5ft (203.76m), length pp 630ft (192m), max beam 62.33ft (19m), mean draft 16.5ft (5m)
Armament	10 x 20cm/50 (5 x 2), 6 x 12cm/45 HA (6 x 1), 2 x 7.7mm Lewis mg, 12 x 24in (61cm) torpedo tubes (4 x 3 fixed; max 36 torpedoes)
Aircraft	2 floatplanes, 1 catapult
Armour	102mm belt (123.15m long x 3.5m height amidships), 35-32mm middle deck, 35mm lower deck. Bulge below belt 93m long x 2.5m max depth
Machinery	Four sets Kampon geared turbines, twelve Kampon water-tube boilers, four shafts, 130,000shp
Fuel capacity	2470 tons
Speed max	35.5 knots
Range	8000nm @ 14 knots
Complement	47 officers, 657 men

Myoko Class Displacement					
	Standard	Displacement $2/3$*	Displacement full load	Belt above waterline amidships	Belt above waterline ends
Design	10,000	12,558	13,256	3.04m	1.54m
As Completed	10,980	13,551	14,662	1.8m	0.30m

* $2/3$ Trial was the Japanese Navy measurement for warship trials. It was full load minus $1/3$ of fuel oil, lubricating oil and reserve feed water

depth. They were to be left as a void but in case of war, watertight steel tubes would occupy the space. Since the cruisers were 12% over designed displacement, other design calculations were out of kilter as well. Draft was increased by almost 4ft (1.2m), so amidships only 6ft (1.8m) of the belt was above the waterline and only 1ft (0.3m) at the bow and stern. In any sort of seaway any battle damage to the hull could entail a significant intake of water.

The ten Type 3 20cm/50 main guns were capable of 40 degrees elevation with a maximum range of 26,700m. The main gun turrets were more gun houses than turrets as they were armoured by only 1in (25.4mm) plates. They were proof against splinters but not against 6in shell strikes. On completion the *Nachi* carried her six 4.7in (120mm) secondary guns in open, hand-operated mounts, but these were quickly replaced with power-operated mounts with gun shields. The catapult was offset to starboard of centreline on the quarterdeck level, just forward of the aft turrets. Although the requirements were for the ship to carry two floatplanes, only one Type 15 seaplane was carried by the ships in the class until November 1932. To reach the designed speed of 35.5 knots a power plant generating 130,000shp was installed. It is interesting to note that the Japanese ran the ships in light condition for their speed trials. Instead of running at the stipulated 2/3 trial displacement, which would have been around 13,300 tons, they were actually tested at a displacement of 12,350 metric tons. This would be far less than their operational displacement, and in this unrealistically light condition all four cruisers attained 35 knots, but only *Nachi* and *Haguro* exceeded the designed 35.5 knots.

Of interest in this photograph is the lack of any superstructure from the hangar just aft of the main mast to the base of No 4 barbette. Also notice the single catapult, covered in natural canvas, which was mounted to the starboard of centreline.

THE *TAKAO* CLASS

Months before the *Myoko*, the lead ship of the class, was laid down, the United States Congress passed a cruiser construction bill that authorised the building of eight 10,000-ton cruisers. Although only the first two, *Pensacola* and *Salt Lake City*, were started immediately, the Japanese Naval General Staff was worried about this large program. Four new 10,000-ton cruisers were part of a new construction request, which was finally approved in March 1927. As originally proposed, these new cruisers were to be additional units of the *Myoko* class but before approval it was decided to construct an improved design. Known as the 'Improved *Myoko*' design, Captain Fujimoto, the Constructor who had finished the *Myoko* design, was again in charge. Improvements over the *Myoko* included increasing the maximum elevation of the main guns to 70 degrees, provision for heavier magazine protection, fitting of two catapults for three floatplanes, rotating torpedo tubes in outboard sponsons instead of fixed mounts within the hull and a huge forward superstructure, reminiscent in appearance of a feudal Japanese castle. One reason for the increase in size of the superstructure was the requirement that all four cruisers be equipped to serve as flagships and the redesigned bridge of the *Takao* class had three times the internal volume of that of the *Myoko*s. The first two were ordered in the 1927 Fiscal Year and the other two in FY 1928.

The hull lines were very similar to the preceding *Myoko* class. Although *Myoko* had been launched the month before, she was far from complete. It was recognised that the improvements in the new design would add weight and, to compensate, welding was used to the maximum extent possible and more aluminium was used. The stipulated 2/3 trial displacement was 12,986 metric tons, but again the systemic design miscalculation came into play and all four cruisers exceeded designed displacement by more than

Takao Class as designed 1927	
Dimensions	Length oa 668.5ft (203.76m), length pp 630ft (192m), max beam 62.33ft (19m), mean draft 16.5ft (5m)
Armament	10 x 20cm/50 (5 x 2), 4 x 12cm/45 HA (4 x 1), 2 x 40mm/62 Vickers AA, 2 x 7.7mm Lewis mg, 8 x 24in (61cm) torpedo tubes (4 x 2 trainable; max 24 torpedoes)
Aircraft	3 floatplanes, 2 catapults
Armour	102mm belt (119.8m long x 3.5m height amidships), 35-32mm middle deck, 35mm lower deck. Bulge below belt 93m long x 2.5m max depth
Machinery	Four sets Kampon geared turbines, twelve Kampon water-tube boilers, four shafts, 130,000shp
Fuel capacity	2645 tons
Speed max	35.5 knots
Range	8000nm @ 14 knots
Complement	47 officers, 679 men

10%. Actual trial displacements ranged from 14,129 to 14,260 metric tons. Any claims that the Japanese did not intentionally violate the terms of the Washington Treaty have to be countered by their continued use of a design system that dramatically under-estimated actual displacement. It did not serve their purposes to correct the system. However, the negative consequences to the cruisers were the same as encountered with those of the Myoko class. The over-weight condition of the Takao class also reduced their freeboard, habitability, speed, range and location of armour belt in relation to the waterline.

The armour belt over machinery spaces was 4in (102mm) with a 12-degree slope, the same as that in the Myoko class. However, the Takao armour plan had the belt cover more vertical distance but was slightly shorter. Maximum thickness was 5in (127mm) for the upper 2.5m of the belt. Because of the extra weight over designed displacement, the main belt extended only a little over 4ft (1.3m) above waterline at trial displacement with the top of the belt at the waterline at the extremities. At full load, the situation was even worse with less than 3ft (0.85m) of the amidships belt above the waterline and the belt extremities submerged. The Takao class also had

the same underwater anti-torpedo bulge that was fitted to the Myoko class.

The Takao carried a new main gun. Designated Type 3 No 2 20cm gun, the actual bore was 203.2mm. This gun had a range of 29,400m at 45 degrees elevation. Although the gun houses were similar to those of the Myoko class with the same armour plates of 25.4mm, they were 5.9in (150mm) higher. The guns were designed to be able to be fired at a maximum elevation of 70 degrees to allow anti-aircraft capabilities for the ordnance, but they proved totally ineffective in that capacity. Instead of having a tight shot grouping, the new guns also spread the salvo to an excessive degree. Since the main guns were expected to also serve in an AA capacity, the secondary 4.7in (120mm) HA guns were reduced to four power-operated shielded mounts from the six mounts fitted on the Myoko class. However, the Takao class did receive some lighter AA ordnance during construction. These amounted to two single Vickers 40mm/62, one mounted on each side of the aft funnel and two single Vickers 7.7mm machine guns, one mounted on each side of the forward funnel. The Vickers 40mm was a short range, low velocity weapon that was replaced in 1935 and is not to be confused with the excellent Bofors 40mm gun of World War Two. With the

Atago went through full power trials on 13 February 1932. During these trials she made 35.2 knots at 135,001shp.

Takao Class Displacement

	Displacement 2/3*	Displacement full load	Belt above waterline amidships	Belt above waterline ends	Range @ 14 knots
Design	12,986	13,700	1.72m	0.42m	8,000nm
As Completed	14,109	15,186	1.3m	0.0m	7,000nm

* 2/3 Trial was the Japanese Navy measurement for warship trials. It was full load minus 1/3 of fuel oil, lubricating oil and reserve feed water

The massive Japanese castle superstructure of the *Chokai* is emphasised in this photograph from 18 June 1938. Although the *Chokai* is at anchor, notice the height of the waves, which would lap over the lower row of scuttles. Due to miscalculation of design weight, the ships of this class were 10% overweight and rode far lower in the water than intended.

Takao class the 61cm rotating torpedo mounts were moved from the locations found in the *Myoko* class. With the *Myoko* design Admiral Hiraga had opposed mounting torpedo tubes above machinery spaces. If a warhead exploded aboard ship, significant, if not catastrophic, damage would be caused. This concern was finally addressed in the *Takao* design. The torpedo tubes were not positioned inside the hull. Instead sponsons, which extended partly beyond the sides of the hull. With rotating mounts the tubes would be swung outward in battle, which would place even more distance between their warheads and the side of the ship.

The *Takao* class was built with two catapults in order to match USN cruiser designs. A small hangar was provided just aft of the mainmast for two of the three seaplanes that were required in the design. Initially, the ships only carried two Type 90 No.2 Model 2 two-seat floatplanes. The machinery requirements for the *Takao* class were basically the same as found in the *Myoko* design. The plant produced the same 130,000shp as the earlier design. Speed trials were conducted under the same lightweight conditions as was done with the *Myoko* class. All four units exceeded 35 knots but only *Chokai* exceeded 35.5 knots without going to overload status.

As built, the cruisers of the *Myoko* and *Takao* classes appear very impressive in their weapon systems and

operational capabilities. To a large degree, this was because the displacement of both classes significantly exceeded the maximum displacement allowed under the Washington Treaty. Whether this was through error - which is hard to believe given the differences in design and actual displacements of the *Yubari*, *Furutaka* and *Aoba* designs – or more likely a deliberate decision to retain a design process that grossly under-estimated displacement, the result was the same. Yet the flawed design process was a two-edged sword. The Japanese Naval General Staff received cruisers more powerful than those in the RN or USN but there were significant penalties. They were slower, with less range, less stable than their designs had calculated and most importantly, with most of their armour belts submerged, they very susceptible to battle damage.

This is *Chokai* on 18 June 1938. She and *Maya* did not undergo the modernisation received by *Atago* and *Takao* and so she retained her mainmast aft of the rear funnel. Shown abreast of the rear funnel is a quadruple 13.2mm Hotchkiss machine gun, which replaced the 40mm Vickers gun by 1937.

Careers

The four cruisers of the *Myoko* class spent most of their careers serving together in the 5th Cruiser Squadron and the four *Takao* class cruisers in the 4th Cruiser Squadron. As the *Myoko* class ships were completed, they were placed in the 4th Cruiser Squadron. On 1 December 1932 they were placed into reserve and in May 1933 became the 5th Cruiser Squadron, as the ships of the *Takao* class were commissioned into the 4th Cruiser Squadron. The *Myokos* were slated for a refit in 1934, so by the fall of 1933 all four were assigned to either the Kure or Sasebo naval bases. *Nachi* and *Haguro* went into the yard in February 1934 and were followed by *Myoko* and *Ashigara* in November. After the refit, the ships of the class again became the 5th Cruiser Squadron. The squadron, less *Ashigara*, supported the Japanese war effort in China in the late 1930s. The ships of the *Takao* class became the 4th Cruiser Squadron from December 1932 and were in service until November 1935. All four were modified to increase hull strength and started going back into operations as the 4th Cruiser Squadron starting December 1936. As all four ships of the *Takao* class were fitted to serve as fleet flagships, they were always in demand.

One of the first independent missions to which a member of the *Myoko* class was assigned involved the *Ashigara*. The cruiser was sent to Great Britain to represent the Imperial Japanese Navy for the Coronation Review for King George VI held on 20 May 1937. This marked the first time in which a member class was examined closely by the western press and naval establishments. When *Ashigara* returned to Japan, she operated independently of her sisters in the waters off Indo-China. She was located in the Pescadore Islands on 7 December 1941, and was part of the Northern Cover Force in the invasion of the Philippine Islands. On 10 December 1941 she was bombed by a USAF B-17 but was not hit. In January 1942 *Ashigara* rejoined her sisters in the 5th Cruiser Squadron.

On 4 January 1942, after supporting landings in the Philippines, the three ships of the 5th Cruiser Squadron were attacked in Malalag Bay from 30,000 feet by ten USAAF B-17s, scoring one of the rare successes of high altitude bombing. One 250-pound bomb struck B turret of *Myoko*, killed 35 and wounded 29 sailors; she was out of action until 26 February 1942. It was in the waters of the Dutch East Indies that these big cruisers finally faced surface opponents.

In May 1937 *Ashigara* represented Japan in the Coronation Review for King George VI. Afterwards she paid a goodwill visit to Germany. In the course of this tour she became the most heavily photographed member of the class.

8

Myoko Class Dates

	Laid Down	Launched	Completed	Fate
Myoko	25 October 1924	16 April 1927	31 July 1929	Scuttled in Malacca Straits on 8 July 1946
Nachi	26 November 1924	15 June 1927	26 November 1928	Sunk by aircraft from USS *Lexington* CV-16, south of Corregidor on 5 November 1944
Haguro	16 March 1925	24 March 1928	25 April 1929	Sunk by torpedoes from British destroyers off west coast of Malaya on 16 May 1945
Ashigara	11 April 1925	22 April 1928	20 August 1929	Sunk by British submarine HMS *Trenchant* off north coast of Sumatra on 7 June 1945

Note: They were built by Yokosuka Navy Yard, Kure Navy Yard, Mitsubishi (Nagasaki) and Kawasaki (Kobe) respectively.

Takao Class Dates

	Laid Down	Launched	Completed	Fate
Takao	28 April 1927	12 May 1930	31 May 1932	Scuttled in Malacca Straits on 27 October 1946
Atago	28 April 1927	16 June 1930	30 March 1932	Sunk by USS *Darter* in Palawan Passage on 22 October 1944
Chokai	26 March 1928	5 April 1931	30 June 1932	Scuttled by destroyer *Fujinami* off of Samar on 25 October 1944
Maya	4 December 1928	8 November 1930	30 June 1932	Sunk by USS *Dace* in Palawan Passage on 22 October 1944

Note: They were built by Yokosuka Navy Yard, Kure Navy Yard, Mitsubishi (Nagasaki) and Kawasaki (Kobe) respectively.

BATTLE OF THE JAVA SEA

The Dutch East Indies were the major prize for which Japan had gone to war. With the pre-war oil embargo against Japan strangling Japanese fuel supplies, the Japanese government saw the capture of the oil fields of Borneo and the Dutch East Indies as essential to make their country self-sufficient. The northern barriers to the Java Sea, Borneo and the Celebes, surrendered in January 1942, and operations against Java and the rest of the Dutch possessions began. The Japanese planned a double envelopment of the islands. The 5th Cruiser Squadron was assigned the mission of covering force for the eastern invasion force.

Opposing the Japanese naval force was a polyglot allied force of American, British, Dutch and Australian warships entitled the ABDA Combined Force. Established on 10 January 1942 ABDA's organisation and communications were appallingly poor and in the event only provided targets for the extremely well prepared and coordinated Japanese attack on the islands. On 3 February 1942 the bulk of the allied warships still operational in the area were placed under the command of Dutch Rear Admiral Karel Doorman.

Nachi was the flagship of Vice Admiral Takeo Takagi, commander of Main Body, Eastern Invasion Support Force. The 5th Cruiser Squadron was down to just *Nachi* and *Haguro*, as *Ashigara* was acting as flagship for Vice Admiral Ibo Takahashi, overall Southern Force commander, and the *Myoko* was at Sasebo for repairs. The eastern invasion force sailed on 19 February but their southward passage was not confirmed by ABDA command until 24 February. Admiral Doorman's strike force consisted of the heavy cruisers HMS *Exeter* and USS *Houston*, the Dutch light cruisers, *Java* and *De Ruyter*, along with HMAS *Perth*. With minimal reconnaissance the allied force started making a series of sweeps in an effort to find Japanese troop convoys, and on 27 February it ran into the Japanese screening forces.

This is the tower bridge of *Haguro* in March 1941. The ship has already taken on a wartime appearance. Canvas dodgers, originally left in natural canvas colour, and the rope-filled canvas bags for additional splinter protection are now dyed a light to mid brown, as were the blast bags for the main guns.

On paper the two forces looked fairly closely matched. In addition to the two heavy and three light cruisers, Doorman's force also had nine destroyers – four American, three British and two Dutch. Facing them were three groups of Japanese forces. One group was the light cruiser *Jintsu* and four destroyers. Another was the light cruiser *Naka* and six destroyers. Furthest north of the Japanese forces were *Nachi* and *Haguro*, along with another four destroyers. However, the allies only had a total of twelve operational 8in guns as *Exeter* had only three twin turrets and *Houston* had only her two forward turrets in operation (*Houston*'s aft turret had been wrecked by a bomb earlier in the month). The forces sighted each other around 15.21 and one of the rarities of the Pacific War occurred: a daylight surface engagement in which aircraft played a minimal role.

In the first of a series of engagements, *Nachi* scored a serious hit on *Exeter* setting her on fire. Two minutes later, a Long Lance torpedo from *Haguro* blew up the Dutch destroyer *Kortenaer*. Doorman turned his force away from the Japanese; the *Exeter*, down to 5 knots and screened by the one Dutch and three British destroyers, separated.

At 17.20 it appeared to Doorman that the Japanese forces were retiring, so he reversed course in another effort to get at the transports, but at 17.28 the Japanese light cruisers with their destroyers altered course towards the *Exeter* group, and the destroyer HMS *Electra* was hit twice and sank at 17.46. The forces lost sight of each other and it appeared that the battle was over. After some time passed, Doorman made his third attempt to find and attack the Japanese troop transports. At 18.50 contact was restored and *Java, Houston, Perth* and *De Ruyter*, with one British and four American destroyers engaged in a harmless skirmish with the Japanese *Nachi, Haguro, Jintsu* and eight destroyers before contact was again broken.

HMS *Jupiter* was lost when she ran into a mine and Doorman detached his four American destroyers to return to port to refuel. So at 22.33 when the *Nachi, Haguro, Jintsu* and eight destroyers regained contact with the allies there were just the *Houston* and three light cruisers left in the allied force. Long range gunfire failed to hit on

either side but then the Japanese fired more torpedoes, eight from *Nachi* and four from *Haguro*. As they would continue to prove through 1942 and 1943, the 24in Japanese Long Lance torpedoes were the battle winners for the Japanese Navy. One hit *De Ruyter* and she soon sank, taking Admiral Doorman with her. In a few minutes another struck *Java* and she quickly followed. The surviving *Houston* and *Perth* broke contact and headed back to Batavia, while the *Exeter, Encounter* and US destroyer *Pope* were at Surabaya.

On the evening of 28 February the *Exeter* force put to sea again with orders to escape to Ceylon. On 1 March the crippled HMS *Exeter* and her two destroyers were trapped between all four members of the *Myoko* class, the *Ashigara* and *Myoko* to the north and the *Nachi* and *Haguro* to the south. Torpedoes from either or both *Nachi* and *Haguro* struck *Exeter* and she sank at 11.30. At 11.35 *Encounter* went down due to hits from *Ashigara* and *Myoko*. The USS *Pope* was the last to

The two forward turrets and the tower bridge of *Haguro* are shown in this photograph from March 1941. The ship has completed her Second Modernisation and the upward slanting yardarms on the new tripod foremast are clearly shown. Under orders to reach peak efficiency by July 1941, Japanese warships significantly changed appearance in this period. Gone were the light natural canvas dodgers and main gun blast bags, which contrasted so smartly with the grey of the paint scheme, in favour of much less visible brown stained canvas.

The struggle for Guadalcanal had just started the month before this photograph of *Atago* in the Solomon Sea was taken in September 1942. A twin 25mm AA mount is shown in the foreground as the cruiser appears to be about to launch a E8N2 Type 95 'Dave' tactical reconnaissance aircraft. The 'Dave' was replaced by the F1M2 Type 0 'Pete' later that year as the standard two-seat floatplane on cruisers. The canvas-covered sisal ropes were intended to offer splinter protection for the searchlights.

go, when she too succumbed to overwhelming fire at around 12.05. The Battle of the Java Sea had lasted two days and was an overwhelming victory for the Japanese Navy. The *Myoko* class cruisers were the key Japanese components in the battle, and although their gunnery at long range had been unimpressive, there is no doubt about the value of their heavy torpedo battery.

Although *Chokai* was with the *Suzuya* and *Kumano* in the 7th Cruiser Squadron, the other three *Takao* class cruisers still made up the 4th Squadron, supporting the western pincer against Java. *Maya* and two destroyers encountered and sank the destroyer HMS *Stronghold* on March 2, and *Takao* and *Atago* sank the old four-stack destroyer USS *Pillsbury*; it took only seven minutes.

BATTLE OF THE CORAL SEA AND THE MIDWAY CAMPAIGN

After their triumphs in the Dutch East Indies, the ships were sent back to the Japanese home islands for quick refits, except *Chokai*, which participated in the raid into the Indian Ocean. Three of the *Myoko*s went back into service in April 1942 but *Ashigara* was not ready until June 1942. In May *Myoko* and *Haguro* were assigned to support the carriers *Zuikaku* and *Shokaku* in the Japanese effort to take Port Moresby, which led to the Battle of the Coral Sea. For the main effort of the Combined

Fleet against Midway in June 1942 *Myoko* and *Haguro* were placed with *Atago* and *Chokai* to support the transports. *Nachi* was selected as flagship 5th Fleet in the Aleutian landings under Vice Admiral Hosogawa. *Takao* and *Maya* were assigned to escort carriers *Junyo* and *Ryujo* in this diversion. During this operation *Takao* managed to shoot down a B-17E. The four cruisers, as part of the Main Force supporting the Midway attack, saw no action.

THE SOLOMON ISLANDS CAMPAIGN

Upon her return from the Midway operation, *Chokai* was selected to be flagship of the newly created 8th Fleet, Outer South Seas Force. Rear Admiral Mikawa Gunichi hoisted his flag aboard the cruiser and steamed off to the Solomon Islands, which he expected to be a backwater. That view changed on 7 August 1942 with the invasion of both Tulagi and Guadalcanal islands by US Marines. The Guadalcanal campaign was to become a gruelling contest of attrition for the next six months and the *Chokai*, as flagship 8th Fleet was there at the start and finish. The *Takao* class as a whole was actively involved in the campaign but the *Myoko* class much less so.

Admiral Mikawa acted immediately in response to the allied landings. He concentrated a force of *Chokai*, the 6th Cruiser Squadron consisting of the four

11

7,500-ton cruisers of the *Furutaka* and *Aoba* classes, two light cruisers and a destroyer. He made quick plans to time his approach in order to arrive at Guadacanal at night. The result was the Battle of Savo Island of early on 9 August, one of the greatest sea victories won by the Imperial Japanese Navy during the war, quickly sinking HMAS *Canberra* and badly damaging USS *Chicago*. Mikawa turned to the north-east and five minutes later attacked the northern allied force of three modern heavy cruisers. USS *Astoria, Quincy* and *Vincennes* were rapidly torn apart and fatally damaged in a cascade of shell and torpedo hits, whereupon Mikawa ordered a retirement. The allies lost four heavy cruisers and over 1,000 men, while the Japanese had 34 men killed, all aboard *Chokai*, which had been hit by three 8in shells.

On 10 August the Japanese High Command ordered the capture of Guadalcanal and it became the business of the Japanese Combined Fleet. On 17 August the 4th Cruiser Squadron of *Takao, Atago* and *Maya* and the 5th Cruiser Squadron of *Myoko* and *Haguro* arrived at Truk. They took part in the Battle of the Eastern Solomons on 24 August, but none of the heavy cruisers was damaged. *Haguro* was dispatched to Sasebo for a refit at the end of September. In October *Chokai, Myoko* and *Maya* were

employed shelling Henderson field. After this *Myoko* was also sent back to Japan for a refit. As flagship of 5th Fleet *Nachi* remained in the north and *Ashigara* spent her time between Singapore and Java except for one troop escort mission to the Shortland Islands.

The naval campaign for Guadalcanal reached its peak in ferocity during three nights in November (13-15th). On the second night of what became known as the Naval Battle of Guadalcanal, the Japanese sent in two cruiser forces comprising *Chokai*, accompanied by *Kinugasa*, and *Maya* and *Suzuya*. The Japanese forces encountered no opposition and freely bombarded Henderson Field, but during the Japanese retirement after daylight, *Kinugasa* was sunk by aircraft from *Enterprise* and *Maya* was damaged. During the attack a Dauntless dive-bomber, hit by AA fire, crashed into the port aft 120mm mount of *Maya*. Resulting fires further cooked off 120mm rounds, causing substantial damage on the port side amidships. *Chokai* had several near misses, which flooded a few compartments but otherwise she remained in fighting trim. *Chokai* was repaired at Truk but *Maya* was sent back to the home islands for repair.

Vice Admiral Kondo saw an opportunity to sweep the remaining allied naval forces from the area the

Except for one escort mission *Ashigara* missed the Guadacanal campaign and remained operating between Singapore and Java. This is *Ashigara* in the King George VI drydock in Singapore on 31 December 1942. On this occasion she was being repainted.

next night. For the battle over 14 to 15 November, Admiral Kondo would take his flagship *Atago*, sister-ship *Takao*, the battleship *Kirishima*, light cruisers and destroyers back to Guadalcanal. The Japanese split their forces into four group but the main body had the two cruisers, the *Kirishima* and two destroyers. *Atago* led, followed by *Takao* and *Kirishima*.

Within the confined waters of The Slot they ran into the battleships *Washington* and *South Dakota* with a destroyer escort. On 14 November 1942, just before midnight, the opposing forces made contact, and the

Atago is leading the other units of the 4th Sentai (*Takao* class) in this photograph from 1942 or 1943. In the foreground is a section of the tripod foremast with the aft funnel and mainmast visible to the rear of that. A E13AI Type 0 'Jake' three-seat long range floatplane is spotted on the starboard catapult. With the huge loss to carrier aircraft at the Battle of Midway the IJN planned to replace all two-seat tactical reconnaissance planes with long-range Jakes, which came into service in the fall of 1942.

This remarkable photograph taken from a USAAF B-25 shows *Haguro* in Rabaul harbour on 2 November 1943 after engaging in the Battle of Empress Augusta Bay early that morning. *Haguro* and *Myoko* had returned to Rabaul after the battle only to be attacked in this raid. Although they suffered no damage in this attack, it became clear that Rabaul was untenable as a forward base.

South Dakota was promptly illuminated by searchlights from *Atago* and *Takao*. At a range of 5,000 yards the Japanese heavies and *Kirishima* concentrated their fire on *South Dakota*. The *Washington* returned fire on the Japanese force but remained unseen. For 30 seconds *South Dakota* was under the glare of the searchlights from the two cruisers before her secondary 5in guns opened up on their source. With this, *Atago* and *Takao* doused their lights and searchlights from *Kirishima* illuminated *South Dakota*.

At least sixteen 8in shells hit the *South Dakota*. Although *Kirishima* was the principal target of the fire of the American battleships, *Atago* received minor damage and *Takao* none. *Kirishima* was doomed when her

rudder was destroyed. The *Washington* was finally seen by the Japanese and Admiral Kondo took *Atago*, *Takao* and the two destroyers after her for a torpedo attack. Luckily for the USN, only the Japanese destroyers fired a few torpedoes at *Washington*, and none hit. Kondo called off the operation and steamed north back to Rabaul.

1943 – BATTLES OF KOMANDORSKI ISLANDS AND EMPRESS AUGUSTA BAY

After the grinding attrition of Guadalcanal, the cruisers of the *Myoko* and *Takao* classes saw a less demanding operational tempo in 1943. All of them returned to home waters for refits during the period, receiving air search radar and augmented light anti-aircraft guns. The *Maya* finished repairing her damages from Guadalcanal at the end of January 1943. She was assigned to join *Nachi* with the 5th Fleet. *Nachi* and *Maya* escorted reinforcements to Attu in the Aleutians from 7 to 13 March and on the 23rd of the month departed on another escort mission. On 27 March 1943 the two cruisers made contact with USS *Salt Lake City* and USS *Richmond* in the Battle of the Komandorski Islands. It became another long-range gunnery duel in daylight, lasting almost four hours, and although *Salt Lake City* was heavily hit, no ships were sunk, although *Maya* fired 904 8in shells and *Nachi* 707 shells. They also launched twenty-four torpedoes, all of which missed at the long range of the engagement. *Nachi* was hit by five 5in shells from *Salt Lake City*, one of which penetrated the forward face of No 1 turret and jammed it.

In October 1943 *Myoko* and *Haguro* were back in Rabaul. On 1 November 1943, while escorting a convoy to

Bougainville, a near miss by a bomb from a B-24 Liberator caused some damage to the bridge and hull of *Haguro*. Within two hours the pair encountered an American Task Force and the result was the Battle of Empress Augusta Bay. Within a space of twenty minutes *Haguro* was hit by ten 6in and 5in shells, although damage was slight. *Myoko* fared worse but not from the enemy. During the battle she collided with an escorting destroyer, and suffered damage as the stricken destroyer passed down the side of the cruiser and tore out two of *Myoko*'s torpedo tubes. Later that morning on 2 November the cruisers were back at Rabaul when they were attacked by USAAF bombers. Although they suffered no further damage, the harbour at Rabaul was becoming untenable due to frequent air attacks. On the morning of 5 November 1943 *Atago* and *Takao* were at anchor at Rabaul when aircraft from USS *Saratoga* attacked them. Three near misses on *Atago* killed 22, including the captain, and injured 64 others. Several compartments were flooded. *Takao* received one hit, which killed 23 men and damaged No 1 and No 2 turrets. *Maya* was also present but she was moving out of the harbour. She was hit on her aircraft deck and a fire started which spread to the engine rooms. She lost 70 killed and 60 wounded. All three were sent back to Japan.

BATTLE OF LEYTE GULF – DEATH OF A CLASS

In response to the allied landings at Leyte Gulf in October 1944, all four members of the *Takao* class and *Haguro* and *Myoko* sailed as part of Admiral Kurita's strong Central Force. *Atago* was Kurita's flagship, as the heavy surface force steamed out of Brunei Bay. Kurita elected to use the Palawan Passage in the approach to the Philippines, where they were attacked by two US submarines, USS *Darter* and USS *Dace* on 22 October. *Darter* targeted Kurita's flagship, the *Atago* leading the left column, and fired all six bow tubes. Then the submarine reversed course and fired the four stern tubes at the second ship in the column, the *Takao*. Five torpedoes hit *Atago* and tore out her port side, while two torpedoes hit *Takao*, destroying the rudder and port drive shafts. The rest of the Japanese fleet then turned to starboard, away from *Darter* but straight towards *Dace*, which let the first two ships in the starboard column (*Myoko* and *Haguro*) past, and selected the third ship. This was misidentified as a battleship but was in fact *Maya*; torpedoes tore open her starboard side and the heavy cruiser was doomed. In a span of minutes two of the *Takao* class were sunk and *Takao* herself badly damaged, although she did manage to limp to safety. Only *Chokai* remained of the class to proceed to Leyte Gulf.

After colliding with *Mogami* in Surigao Strait early on 25 October 1944, the damaged *Nachi* reached Manila Bay and was still there on 5 November. *Nachi* desperately manoeuvres to avoid an attack by aircraft from USS *Lexington* (CV-16) on that day, three miles south of Corregidor.

Two days later Kurita, who had survived the sinking of *Atago* was now on *Yamato*, with his force in the Sibuyan Sea, south of Luzon. On 24 October Kurita's fleet was subjected to wave after wave of aerial attacks from Halsey's carriers. Although *Musashi* was the main target, other ships were hit in the American attacks. *Myoko* was hit by a torpedo, and with her speed reduced to 15 knots, *Myoko* struggled to the rear and was ordered to return westward to Borneo. The flag of the 5th Cruiser Squadron, now comprising one ship, was transferred to *Haguro*. Halsey thought that Kurita's force had become combat ineffective as a result of these aerial attacks and decided to steam north after the bait offered by Admiral Ozawa's diversionary force of aircraft carriers, which allowed Kurita's force to pass through the San Bernardino and attack Leyte Gulf from the north.

The other two ships of the *Myoko* class had started in Chinese waters. Under Vice Admiral Shima, *Nachi*, *Ashigara*, the light cruiser *Abukuma* and three destroyers made towards the southern entrance to the Surigao Strait. Their mission was to support *Fuso*, *Yamashiro* and *Mogami* under Admiral Nishimura in forcing the Surigao Strait and attacking shipping within Leyte Gulf from the south. As Shima steamed up the strait, the remnants of Nishimura's force were scrambling back southward. Only *Mogami* was left of the heavy ships. On fire but still making 8 knots, she was sighted by *Nachi*, which was Shima's flagship and leading the column. From *Nachi*, *Mogami* was thought to be dead in water. It was not until *Nachi* was close aboard *Mogami* that it was realised that the tough *Mogami* was still under way. By then it was too late and *Nachi* embedded her

bow into the already stricken *Mogami*. As she broke free, *Nachi* left part of her bow still wedged in the side of the other cruiser. At first Shima wanted to continue north but considering the fate of Nishimura's heavier force and the fact that *Nachi* was now reduced to 20 knots speed, Shima retired to the south without making contact with allied ships. *Ashigara* and the damaged *Nachi* made for Manila Bay.

On the morning of 25 October 1944 Kurita's force encountered the escort

carriers of 'Taffy 3' under Rear Admiral Clifton Sprague. From the start of the action the Japanese heavy cruisers were among the more effective units in Kurita's force and aggressively closed with the Americans. *Haguro* and *Chokai* formed a two-ship column with the battleships *Kongo* and *Haruna* to port and the battleships *Yamato* and *Nagato* to starboard. The *Haguro* fired at 06.05 but was delayed in closing the Americans by desperate aerial attacks. At 07.41 *Haguro* and *Chokai* started hitting the escort carrier *Gambier Bay*. Then *Haguro* was subjected by torpedo attacks from the destroyers *Hoel* and *Heerman*. The torpedoes were evaded but at 07.51 *Haguro* was hit by a shell,

This is the end of *Nachi*. In the attack of 5 November 1944 *Nachi* was hit by nine torpedoes, twenty bombs and rocket fire from the aircraft. Here she is in her death throes, as the bow has already been blown off and sunk. The aft magazines have detonated and the sinking stern can be seen separated from amidships section of the hull.

This unusual photograph seems to portray *Takao* as she was at Singapore at the end of the war. Never repaired after being torpedoed in October 1944, she, like *Myoko*, was a floating AA battery at Singapore. Although of poor quality, this photo indicates that *Takao* was given a camouflage paint scheme at Singapore.

which caused her to fall out of line. *Chokai* was suffering even worse damage. Hit many times and with holes in her bow, speed dropped off quickly for *Chokai*. Finally the Japanese flagship at the Battle of Savo Island was dead in the water. The crew was evacuated and *Chokai* sunk by torpedoes from the destroyer *Fujinami*. The *Takao* class had ceased to exist as operational units of the Imperial Japanese Navy. *Atago*, *Maya* and *Chokai* were sunk and *Takao*, minus her stern, made it safely to Singapore. She was never repaired and became a stationary anti-aircraft platform. *Takao* was attacked by British submarines at Singapore on 31 July 1945 but was not sunk. After the war, she served briefly as an accommodation hulk until being taken out and scuttled in the Malacca Strait on 27 October 1946.

The first of the *Myoko* class to succumb was the *Nachi*. After losing her bow at Surigao Strait in her collision with *Mogami*, she had safely made it to Manila Bay but on 5 November 1944 was discovered by aircraft from USS *Lexington* near Corregidor. In an incredibly savage attack, the hull of *Nachi* was blown into three parts. *Nachi* has hit by nine torpedoes, twenty bombs and rocket fire from the aircraft. *Ashigara* was not damaged during this attack but clearly remaining at Manila would invite further attack and she steamed for Singapore.

Haguro had survived the Battle of Leyte Gulf and returned to Singapore. In a supply mission to the Andaman Islands, she was sunk by torpedoes from five British destroyers in a perfectly executed flotilla attack on 16 May 1945. *Ashigara*'s turn came the next month, during a regular run between Singapore and Java ferrying

air crews and mechanics. On 7 June 1945 around noon the British submarine HMS/M *Trenchant* spotted *Ashigara* moving northward in the Banka Strait at 15 knots and fired six torpedoes at 4,600 yards. After five hit in a space of six seconds *Ashigara*'s captain tried to beach her in shoal water but she capsized at 12.39.

That left only the lead ship, the *Myoko*. After being knocked out of the line by a torpedo at Sibuyan Sea in October, *Myoko* had made it back to Singapore. Her damage was repaired

and she went back into operation. However, on 12 December 1944, while operating off Indochina, she was hit by a torpedo from the submarine USS *Bergall*. Like the *Takao*, she was towed back to Singapore and never repaired. She remained here as a stationary AA barge until the end of the war. On 8 July 1946 *Myoko* was towed into the Malacca Straits and scuttled.

This is a post-war photograph of *Myoko* at Singapore. Officers of the Royal Navy can be seen departing the ship. She still wears the light and dark grey camouflage that was applied at Singapore in 1945. Note the circular steel plate welded to one of the hull scuttles. In November to December 1943 during her Second Wartime Modification, the *Myoko* had all of her lower row of scuttles plated over as well as some on the middle deck.

Myoko on 25 September 1945. The two-tone or perhaps three-tone camouflage scheme was applied to *Myoko* after she lost her stern to a torpedo strike on 12 December 1944 from USS *Bergall*. She was towed back to Singapore but was never repaired. She served as a floating AA battery.

Model Products

BIRTH OF A WORLDWIDE STANDARD

As the decade of the 1960s closed commercially produced warship models presented no clear standard scale in the world marketplace. In the United Kingdom Airfix used 1:600 scale for their warship models and Frog used 1:500 scale. On the continent the French firm of Heller popularised 1:400 scale for their warship kits. In the United States scales were something found on fish, not in warship models. True, Aurora produced ship kits said to be in a constant 1:600 scale and Renwal had kits in 1:500 scale but the largest producer, Revell, was all over the map. Warship kits from Revell were produced in *box scale*, in that models were designed to fit into standard sized boxes rather than producing boxes to fit models in a constant scale. The situation in Japan was equally confused, with a bewildering variety of scales used by the different manufacturers. The world of warship model design and production radically changed at the start of the 1970s when a consortium of four Japanese manufacturers agreed to produce models in the constant scale of 1:700. Aoshima, Hasegawa, Fujimi and Tamiya divided the warships of the Imperial Japanese Navy of World War Two among themselves and produced a line of model warships breathtaking in the comprehensive coverage of the ships of the IJN - and all in 1:700 scale and a waterline format. Prior to that massive waterline series, almost all warship kits were produced as full-hull models. A full-hull model has the underwater portion of the hull, as well as the structure above. The new series did away with the underwater portion of the hull and replicated the ships as they would appear in the water. The waterline 1:700 scale model warship has become the most popular format of warship model and de facto world standard. Another by-product of this decision was the popularisation of Japanese warship kits on the world market. Prior to the formation of this consortium, it was rare to find a model of a Japanese warship outside of Japan. If you wanted one, you would have to find one of the few importers of the Japanese kits. In Europe no major company produced a model of a Japanese warship, although the British firm of Eaglewall did have 1:1200 scale plastic models of *Yamato* and *Zuikaku* in their line. In the United States only Aurora produced a Japanese warship kit, again the *Yamato*. With the formation of the consortium and production of 1:700 scale waterline models, the Japanese firms exported their kits to the world market and greatly expanded the interest of the world's modellers in the designs of the warships of the Imperial Japanese Navy. From the start the *Myoko* and *Takao* class heavy cruisers were among the favourites with modellers outside of Japan.

For the *Myoko* and *Takao* class cruisers, the widest variety of models for the ships is in waterline 1:700 scale by the Japanese manufacturers. However, the largest size models readily available at the present time are the models of the two classes in 1:500 scale produced by Nichimo. The firm of Konishi does produce huge 1:200 scale resin and metal models of both classes but at a price of 243,000 yen (US$2,000/£1,200 sterling), the price tag is far beyond the means of the average modeller. This situation should change in the future as the US firm of Yankee Modelworks is planning on producing resin and metal models of at least one of these classes in 1:350 scale by the end of 2006.

Metal Collectors or Wargaming Scales

Several firms produce models of the *Myoko* and *Takao* classes in 1:1250 and 1:1200 scales. Neptun of Germany produces extraordinarily well-detailed models of both classes in 1:1250 scale. For their size they really are incredible models. Currently produced is one version of the *Myoko* class: the *Nachi* in her 1943 fit (N1233). However, for the *Takao* class Neptun produces three unique models, all in their 1944 fit. The *Maya* (N1232a) depicts the cruiser in her four-turret configuration. The *Atago* (N1232) depicts the *Atago* and *Takao* with wide spaced masts. The *Chokai* (N1232b) depicts this cruiser with the narrow spaced masts. All of these models come pre-assembled and painted in a dark grey with highlights in brown, black and brass, although the decks are in the same dark grey as the hull, rather than with the unique red-brown linoleum decks.

In the United States Superior produces 1:1200 scale models of both

classes. The Superior line marketed by Alnavco is the direct descendant of aerial recognition models produced during World War Two for the United States Navy. The Superior models lack the fineness of detail of the Neptun models. They come unpainted with the turrets separate from the hull casting. However, the line is very popular with tabletop wargamers, as they are far less susceptible to damage from handling than the delicate Neptun versions, as well as being available at less than half the price of their German cousins. For wargamers with limited space, GHQ and C in C produce 1:2400 scale unpainted models of both classes.

All Neptun Samples: Neptun/Navis

The two outside models are both *Nachi*, Neptun 1233. These offer a nice comparison to the two inside models. *Maya*, Neptun N1232a, is the second from the bottom and reflects her conversion as an AA cruiser in 1944. The *Atago*, N1232, also portrays the ship as she and *Takao* appeared in 1944.

This magnified photograph of the bridge of the Neptun *Maya*, N1232a, emphasises the major changes made to the ship in her refit as an AA cruiser. Gone is the third 8in gun turret and in its place is a deckhouse, three triple 25mm AA mounts and another two twin 127mm DP mounts. This is the ship's appearance at the time of her loss in the Palawan Passage in October 1944.

Far left: This magnified photograph of the Neptun *Atago* 1944, N1232, shows the incredible detail worked into these amazing models; including the many 25mm guns added in the Second Wartime Modification.

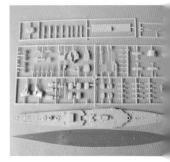

Hasegawa: *Ashigara* 1:700 Scale, 1972 Version

This model is one of the original wave of releases of the 1:700 scale waterline series. Hasegawa had the rights in the consortium for production of models of the *Myoko* class. Marketed by Hasegawa's US distributor, Mini Craft, the US $2.00 retail price made the kit affordable with almost any warship modeller. The model was revolutionary

in 1972 but is very dated by today's standards. All four ships of the *Myoko* class were marketed but the only difference among the models appears to be the name and box art, as the models within the boxes seem to be identical. The *Ashigara* kit does not mention any year as to the fit but clearly is in her late-war appearance, suggested by the presence of triple 25mm mounts on the forecastle and quarterdeck. The hull sides are generally accurate but the

The contents of the 1972 Hasegawa release of *Ashigara* may look spartan now but at that time the kit represented a great leap in bringing models of the class to all of the world's modellers outside of the Japanese home market.

sheer of the cutwater appears to be slightly exaggerated. Detail is rather basic. The lines of the torpedo bulge look correct but none of the vertical strakes that appeared on the bulges are present and the hull lacks the lower row of portholes forward (but the lower row was plated over by early 1944). There are also some problems presented in the plan view, with the shape and position of bollards and their base plates. Although the kit has all four triple 25mm and eight twin 25mm mounts, it does not have any of the 22 single 25mm mounts. Detail and shape of the 25mm mounts is rather sparse and off in appearance and the gun shields for the 5in mounts do not have the asymmetrical shape of that weapon system. The upper deck of the tower bridge is far too narrow for a late-war fit. Still, by 1972 standards the 95 parts found in the box presented a kit of significant complexity. No longer in production, this kit still can be found at model shows. However, the greatest appeal of this groundbreaking product should be for collectors.

Sample: Author's Collection

Aoshima: *Takao* 1:700 Scale, 1994 Version

Among the four companies of the consortium, Aoshima had the rights to production of the *Takao* class cruisers. By 1994 the kits had been out for two decades and were starting to show their age. As an upgrade measure Aoshima introduced the 'Leviathan' edition for these cruiser kits. The models still came with the original 1970s parts but in addition two new identical sprues of parts were added containing new parts for small fittings. This particular kit does not state the year represented but the fittings on the hull clearly show that it is 1944. The hull sides have the basic lines, such as the torpedo bulge but all of the smaller details found on the bulges are not present. Location for the torpedo mounts on each side are merely insets with no tube parts. The kit designers also missed the exact contour of the cutwater.

The deck plan view reflects rather good detail for the period, but the greatest failure of the kit is to omit all single 25mm anti-aircraft guns. This is significant, as there were 30 of these guns on the ship in the 1944 fit. Although the kit supplies all of the twin and triple 25mm gun mounts, these parts are over-scale with extremely thick barrels. To counter this Aoshima provided Leviathan upgrades starting in 1994. These two identical frets provided replacement parts for the twin 25mm, triple 25mm, 5in secondary armament, ship's boats, searchlights and signal lamps, catapults, directors, and floatplanes. This upgrade set was placed in all kits of Japanese cruiser and battleship subjects, so there are parts that do not apply to *Takao*. With the two upgrade frets the modeller is provided a nice selection of Japanese floatplanes used during the war: two each of the 'Alf', 'Dave', and 'Pete', and one 'Jake'. All of the Leviathan upgrade parts were significantly better in quality and detail than the original parts found in the kit. Even with the additional new parts, some of the original defects were not cured. The main gun turrets still had barrel parts without blast bags coming through grossly over-sized openings in the turret front face. The kit contained 107 original parts, along with 166 upgrade parts found in the Leviathan sprues, although not all are used. This kit is a very interesting link between the early waterline kits of the class and the current, completely new models of the ships in the class.

Sample: Courtesy Trident Hobbies

Very much like the original *Takao* receiving a refit to improve her capabilities, this 1995 Aoshima release did the same thing in 1:700 scale. The hull and the sprue on the left are still present from the original 1972 release but the Leviathan sprue on the right was added in this release to provide far greater detail in armament, fittings and aircraft. In this photograph the dramatic improvement made by the new sprues is clearly depicted in a contrast of the 25mm AA mounts in both sprues.

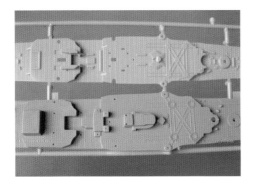

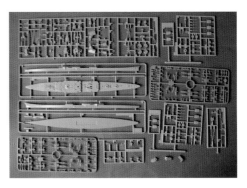

Hasegawa: *Haguro* 1:700 Scale New Tooling

This kit is the current state of the art for 1:700 scale models of the *Myoko* class. This 2001 model is completely reworked from the 1972 Hasegawa release - even 'reworked' is an understatement, as the model is entirely new, with one exception: the decision to continue supplying the Leviathan frets developed seven years earlier to upgrade the old kits. Emphasising the complexity of the new kit compared with the old *Ashigara*, the new version has 131 parts, plus the same 166 parts found on the two Leviathan upgrade sets, contrasted with the 95 parts in the original model. Hasegawa provides optional parts in the box to allow the modeller to build either of two fits. What the instructions call the 'Second Refitting' occurred in the four ships from 1939 to 1941 so this fit reflects the ships in their late 1941 or early 1942, Battle of the Java Sea configuration. There is also a 'final service configuration' option - clearly the late-war 1945 version with all of the additional twin and triple 25mm AA mounts. The 22 single 25mm AA mounts are still not provided in the kit, but, if you flip the deck over, you will see that Hasegawa has placed locator holes on the deck bottom for all light AA weapons, and it is a simple matter to use a pin-vice to drill these out. However, for late-war versions, further research should be conducted for the exact placement of the AA guns, as not all ships used the same positions.

Beyond a simple parts count, the 2001 Hasegawa kit is far superior to their 1972 kit. Instead of a one-piece hull and deck, the New Tool kit provides two hull halves and a separate deck. All of the smaller fittings on the torpedo bulge, the bottom row of portholes, a much more accurate cutwater, far superior torpedo mount/catapult sponsons and much greater detail marked on the hull sides, show it to be a much better and accurate kit than the earlier version. What is especially impressive is the number of optional parts to differentiate the late 1941 fit from the 1945 fit, including a completely different bridge design and a great number of anti-aircraft guns. Other optional parts are both masts and searchlight tower configurations. Hasegawa provides the modeller a lot of highly detailed, quality parts with this new model of the *Haguro*.

Sample: Courtesy Trident Hobbies

Far left: The difference in detail between the original 1972 Hasegawa kit and the new 2001 Hasegawa *Myoko* class kit is readily apparent in this photograph. The new deck at the top has far greater detail, including the grid pattern on the non-ckid motal deck around X barbette, than found on the deck of the 1972 release at the bottom.

Above right: Another strong contrast between the 1972 Hasegawa *Myoko* class release and the company's 2001 release of models of the same class is the proliferation of parts. Not only are the individual parts of the new release far more detailed than the comparable parts in the older kit, but parts count has more than tripled with the 2001 release. This photograph shows the box contents for the Hasegawa 2001 *Haguro* release.

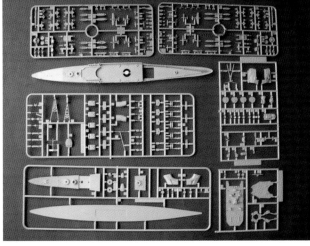

The contents of the new Aoshima *Atago* 1942 fit. The new kit still utilises the Leviathan frets introduced in 1994 and found at the top of the photograph. All other parts are completely new for this release.

A contrast between the original Aoshima kit and the new Aoshima *Takao* class kit is seen here. The deck at top is from the original release and although it is for a 1944 fit, the lack of detail in contrast to the deck of the new Aoshima kit at the bottom is obvious.

Aoshima: *Atago* 1942 Fit, 1:700 Scale New Tooling

As the largest and probably the most popular class of Japanese heavy cruiser, the *Takao*s class have received the greatest attention from kit manufacturers. Furthermore, depending upon the year of the fit, each of the four vessels has details that are unique to that ship. As with the Hasegawa kits of the *Myoko*s, Aoshima has produced completely new models of the *Takao* class. This class has always had a major appearance difference between models of *Atago* and *Takao* with the mainmast aft of the aircraft deck and *Chokai* and *Maya* with the mainmast forward of it. However, Aoshima has gone further and made each model unique. The *Atago* replicates the 1942 fit, as at Midway; the *Takao* is in her 1944 state (as at Leyte); *Chokai* shows her 1942 appearance at the Battle of Savo Island; and *Maya* is in her 1944 fit with only four turrets. Aoshima produces a fifth 1:700 scale model of this class, which is the 1944 *Maya* with the addition of photo-etch parts. Finally, someone got the complex curve of the cutwater correct, and the detail is far greater in this completely new kit than found in the earlier Aoshima effort. As with the Hasegawa New Tool *Myoko* class cruisers, these New Tool

Takao class kits retained the 1994 Leviathan upgrade sprues for the small fittings. There are 100 parts, along with the 166 parts found on the Leviathan frets.

Detail on the one-piece hull/ quarterdeck part is excellent as there are discernible plate lines, bulge detail, both rows of portholes and enhanced hull side detail. The openings for the torpedo mounts are covered by a slight film of plastic, easily opened with a hobby knife. Aoshima includes some parts that would be common to all four ships in the class but also includes specific ship-fit sprues. One common sprue contains the forecastle and stack, but the section of the deck for C or No 3 turret is a separate part, to accommodate the section of extra AA guns needed for the *Maya* 1944 fit. Unlike the original kits of the ships in this class, separate 8in guns with nice blast bag detail is included for the all-new turrets. The Aoshima New Tool 1942 fit *Atago* is an excellent kit with plenty of detail for the modeller and could also be used for the *Takao* as of 1942. Aoshima also produces a *Chokai* in her 1942 Battle of Savo Island fit, which would also be suitable for *Maya* in 1942.

Sample: Courtesy Pacific Front Hobbies

Skywave: *Atago* 1941 Fit, 1:700 Scale

Skywave is another Japanese company, but was not part of the original consortium. They produce five of their own 1:700 scale models of the *Takao* class. *Atago* is in her 1941 fit, after modernisation but still with her original 120mm single gun HA mounts. *Takao* comes in two versions, as separate kits are made of her 1942 and 1944 fits. The *Chokai* and *Maya* kits are both of their 1944 versions, but of course the 1944 *Maya* is unique in having only four 8in gun turrets. The Skywave *Atago* is completely different in design from the New Tool Aoshima *Atago*. Skywave chose to mould the hull with separate starboard and port sides and four deck parts. Skywave does not use the 1994 Leviathan upgrade sprue used by the other consortium companies, but has produced its own version that provides a substantial improvement over the parts included in the New Tool Hasegawa *Myoko* class and New Tool Aoshima *Takao* class kits. Skywave includes the single 25mm AA guns with detailed base plates so conspicuously absent in the Hasegawa and Aoshima kits. There are two of these sprues in the kit so the modeller receives a total of 30 single 25mm mounts. These single 25mm guns are not used in the 1941 fit *Atago* but of course make a tremendous difference in kits for late-war fits. Also on this sprue are five seaplanes. The same four types of aircraft are provided as on the Leviathan sprue with the addition of a second 'Dave'. With a total of ten floatplanes included in this one kit, you will certainly have plenty of spares left. The fineness and detail of the Skywave aircraft and ship's boats has the edge over comparable Aoshima parts but the Aoshima double and triple

25mm AA guns edge their Skywave contemporaries.

The Skywave hull halves have very nice detail with the complex curve of the cutwater, two rows of portholes and horizontal panel lines of the hull captured. However, the Skywave torpedo bulges do not have the detail included in the Aoshima version. Separate decks are provided for the forecastle, quarterdeck, torpedo/quarterdeck, and aircraft deck. Since both *Takao* kits, Aoshima and Skywave, are of the early-war fit *Atago*, a direct comparison is possible. The front face of the forward superstructure in the Skywave *Atago* has substantially more detail than that found in the Aoshima kit. Almost all of the Skywave smaller parts are very well done. On the whole the edge in detail goes to Skywave over Aoshima but with certain parts, such as the torpedo bulge detail and 5in gun shields, the Aoshima parts are better. However, the modeller would be well served with either the Skywave or Aoshima New Tool kit, with the exception of late-war fits, where the inclusion of single 25mm AA guns makes the Skywave kit much more suitable.

Sample: Courtesy Trident Hobbies

Bottom: The excellent hull and superstructure detail of the Skywave *Atago* 1941 fit kit is evident. Clean, deep scuttles, open hull cut-outs for the 610mm torpedo tubes, and fine door detail are just examples of the high quality of this kit.

Below: This photograph emphasises the detail of the main gun mounts. Notice not only crown detail but also that gun barrels have blast bags with individual folds. The hull also reflects great detail. The lower row of scuttles indicates an early to mid-war appearance. The Second Wartime refit in late 1943 plated over these scuttles.

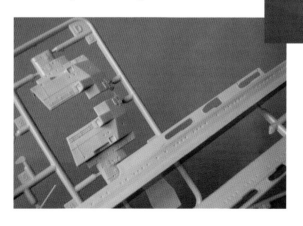

Nichimo: *Nachi* 1:500 Scale

This kit was produced in the 1970s but production stopped around 1984. However, with the absence of any new models of the class larger than 1:700 scale, it has been brought back into production. Nichimo markets models of all four ships of the class but after examination of all four, there appears to be no difference among them other than their names and artwork on the box. The size difference over the 1:700 scale models is considerable. The Nichimo *Nachi* has a red lower hull as well. However, the lower hull is designed for motorisation with an over-size rudder and only one centreline shaft. Nichmo does provide shafts and propellers to replace the motorised parts for a scale static full-hull build. Although Nichimo also makes 1:500 scale kits of the four *Takao* class cruisers, the Nichimo *Myoko* class kits are significantly superior in detail. Therefore, any of these four kits is the best affordable source for a large model of the Japanese cruisers of the *Myoko* or *Takao* classes. The Nichmo kit portrays the class after the addition of torpedo bulges and change in floatplane deck rails in the 1939 to 1941 refit. This kit best shows the class as they appeared at the Battle of the Java Sea. Nichimo includes a radar for a 1944 fit but the kit does not have other parts to support this fit. Significant modifications would be required to make this kit a model of a late-war *Myoko* class, especially for the bridge levels and light AA complement.

Deck detail is adequate but some fittings are overdone and over-scale, but there is nothing here that cannot be fixed. A more serious error is found on the floatplane flight deck. Nichimo shows this area to be a metal deck and yet photographs clearly show the same linoleum deck panels as found on the forecastle and quarterdeck. Nichimo

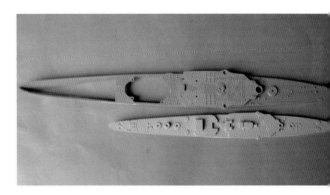

includes the two styles of turrets used for the main guns, as No 1, No 2 and No 4 turrets had a small step down with vision or ventilation holes, which did not appear on turrets No 3 and No 5. The barrels lack blast bags. The kit contains two floatplanes that appear to represent the Type 0 E13A1 'Jake'. It is charitable to call them adequate, but compared with what Nichimo provides with the *Takao* class kits, they are perfection personified. The bridgework appears to follow the 1942 fit until you reach the upper directors. Nichimo provides a single director, as in the 1944 fit, rather than two directors in the 1942 fit. In spite of the problems with this kit, it is the best larger platform for the modeller and is amenable to significant improvement through the use of commercially available photo-etch products and some comparatively minor alterations.

Sample: Courtesy Trident Hobbies

Why are the Nichimo 1:500 scale models so appealing in spite of their age? The answer can be seen in this photograph. At 1:500 scale, the Nichimo *Nachi* hull at top is far larger than the 1:700 Hasegawa *Ashigara*, 1972 release, hull at the bottom.

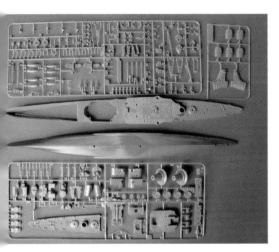

Without a doubt the Nichimo models of the *Myoko* class cruisers are much better in quality than the same company's *Takao* class kits. Although it has significant faults, this Nichimo kit of *Nachi* allows the average modeller to build a large, impressive replica of the ship without investing half a lifetime in making corrections.

妙高型はワシントン軍縮条約の制限１万トン以内で、最大性能を発揮させようとした平賀造船将官の名艦で、第二次大戦で大活躍した１万トン級重巡の基礎を築いたものといえます。那智は昭和３年に呉海軍工廠で竣工し、昭和11年に第一次改装、昭和16年に第二次改装が完成開戦前には最新鋭重巡と同程度の性能をもっていました。改装完成後の主要目は、基準排水量13千トン、速力33.8ノット、20センチ連装６基10門、12.7センチ連装４基８門、61センチ４連装発射管４基16門、呉式水上偵察機１基、零式観測機２機です。

那智が参加した作戦は、開戦と同時に第５戦隊の１艦としてセレベス方面攻略作戦に参加、17年１月４日旗艦妙高の被爆により旗艦となる。昭和17年２月27日のスラバヤ沖海戦では羽黒と協同してイギリスの重巡エクセターを撃破する。昭和17年４月６日第５戦隊旗艦を妙高に移し、北方部隊の旗艦となって北方作戦を支援。昭和18年３月27日アッツ島沖海戦に参加、昭和７月30日まで北方作戦を支援する。昭和19年７月31日機動部隊に編入される。捷一号作戦でフィリピン沖海戦に第２遊撃隊として参加。11月５日マニラ湾に待機中、敵機動部隊の集中攻

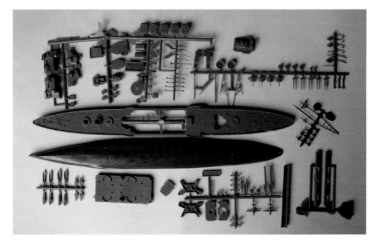

Nichimo: *Maya* 1:500 Scale

The 1:500 scale models of the *Takao* class are much rougher in appearance than the company's kits of the *Myoko* class. Most egregious are the solid deck railings that resemble concrete highway dividers. Still, these kits are the only readily available large size models of the class. With skill and patience, even these old war-horses can be reworked into very attractive models. Unlike the Nichimo models of the *Myoko* class, the firm's *Takao* class models present two different kits, based upon mast arrangement. The *Atago* and *Takao* kits are identical, with mainmast aft of the aircraft deck from the 1939 refit. The *Maya* and *Chokai* kits are identical, with mainmast forward of the aircraft deck, since they never went to the yard for the refit received by the other two. The *Maya* kit is with five turrets, so it is not in her 1944 fit. The lower hull is designed for motorisation with an over-size rudder and only one centreline shaft. However, unlike the Nichimo *Myoko* class kits, there are no substitute parts of shafts or propellers for a static build of the kit.

The hull represents the unmodified lines of the class as originally built, without torpedo bulges, and the cutwater lacks the proper complex curve. The decks are sparse and lacking in detail, and on the main gun turrets most crown detail is absent. This kit does come with four 4.7in guns in gun shields for the *Maya* before her 1943 refit, but the kit part is symmetrical, rather than asymmetrical as the original, the plan view is wrong and the side profile does not come close. The forward superstructure seems to follow the 1937 appearance of the tower bridge but the Nichimo kit places the widest point of the bridge face one level too high. The adjective 'abysmal' comes to mind in describing the two floatplanes included with the kit.

The box art of the Nichimo versions of *Takao* and *Atago* show the 1939 ships after refit with significant torpedo bulges and mainmast moved further aft. Odds are, these two kits will be even further afield in accuracy than the *Maya* and *Chokai*. So, after reading this litany of woe, why would a modeller want to build one of the Nichimo *Takao* class kits? It is the only game in town, the only affordable large-scale model for this class – but they will take significantly more effort to upgrade than the Nichimo *Myoko* class kits.

Sample: Courtesy Trident Hobbies

Above right: The superstructure parts of the Nichimo *Maya* reflect the 20+ years that the kit has been in production. The scuttles are far too large, the riveting and platform supports are too heavy, and there is an injection mark on the exterior surface. However, far more fundamental, the superstructure has the wrong cross section.

Above left: The contents of the 1:500 scale Nichimo *Maya* are seen in this photograph. Even here the features found along the deck edges appear more representative of solid concrete highway dividers than of railing. However, in spite of the kit's drawbacks, it is the only readily affordable model of a *Takao* class cruiser larger than 1:700 scale.

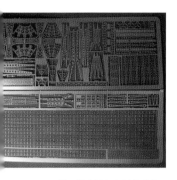

The Gold Medal Models fret contains parts for many different classes of Japanese cruiser, as well as some items for destroyers.

Above: This is the Gold Medal Model photo-etch fret in 1:500 scale for Japanese cruisers and destroyers. It is of the same design as the 1:700 scale fret on the same topic. One benefit of this particular fret is that it includes railing

Right: Detailed aircraft cradles can be added to the flight decks of your 1:700 scale *Myoko* and *Takao* class cruisers through the Tom's Model-works photo-etch fret for cruisers of the IJN

Below: Tom's Modelworks 1:500 scale brass photo-etch fret has the advantage of being designed solely for IJN cruisers but does not include railings.

Gold Medal Models

Loren Perry, who runs Gold Medal Models, is from Lopez, Washington. GMM is one of the top photo-etch producers in the world and has an extensive line of products for the modeller. One characteristic of Gold Medal Models is the production of a 'type' photo-etch fret. That is seen in these two products for IJN Cruisers/ Destroyers as types. Both frets provide a wide variety of parts for almost each class of Japanese heavy cruiser, some for Japanese light cruisers and some for Japanese destroyer kits. Designed in the mid-1990s, the two sets listed below do not have relief-etching found in the sets designed by Gold Medal Models at the present.

GMM 500-3

This fret measures 6 inches by 5 inches. It is an enlarged 1:500 scale version of the 1:700 scale Japanese cruisers/ destroyers fret from Gold Medal Models and has the same specific parts for the Nichimo 1:500 scale kits of the *Myoko* and *Takao* classes as mentioned for the 1:700 kits. Photo-etch products in this scale are very rare.

Sample: Courtesy Gold Medal Models

GMM 700-13

This fret measures 4 inches by 3 inches and is packed with stainless steel parts for modellers. As a 'type' set, it covers a wide range of classes, but for the *Myoko* class specific parts are present for the catapults, aircraft crane, searchlight towers, radar, aircraft trolleys and turret crown tripods. For the *Takao* class models, the modeller receives catapults, aircraft crane, aircraft trolleys and radar. The fret also comes with a generous supply of railing, vertical ladder and inclined ladder.

Sample: Courtesy Gold Medal Models

Tom's Modelworks

Tom's Modelworks, run by Tom Harrison, is also one of the big names in the world of photo-etch detail parts for the naval modeller. Tom's produces type sets specifically for Japanese heavy cruisers in 1:700 scale and 1:500 scale.

Tom's Modelworks 1/500 Scale IJN Heavy Cruiser, Set #5003

This fret is a scaled up version of the Tom's Modelworks 1:700 scale photo-etch set on Japanese heavy cruisers. As such the parts mix provided for the Nichimo kits in 1:500 scale are the same. One disadvantage of this particular fret is that it does not include a 1:500 fret of railing, inclined ladder and vertical ladder.

Sample: Courtesy Tom's Modelworks

Tom's Modelworks 1/700 Scale IJN Heavy Cruiser, Set #726

This set has the advantage of being designed only for Japanese heavy cruisers, but it does have parts for the *Furutaka, Aoba, Mogami* and *Tone* classes alongside items for the *Myoko* and *Takao* classes. This set comes with two frets. One, measuring 5 inches by slightly under 2 inches, contains structural parts for the ships. Parts specifically designed or usable for Hasegawa *Myoko* class cruisers are the aircraft crane, catapults, aircraft cradles, aircraft trolleys, aircraft propellers, searchlight tower, air search radar Type 21, turret tripod antennae, anchors, and RDF loops. For the *Takao* class cruisers, parts include the same items but with a different aircraft crane and no searchlight platform. The second fret, measuring 5 inches by 1 inch contains mostly two-bar railing. Also included is a run of inclined ladder and vertical ladder, which must be cut to the correct lengths.

Sample: Courtesy Tom's Modelworks

Voyager Model

This company, based in Shanghai, China is a newcomer to the realm of warship model photo-etch. However, their products present items and features not seen before. Rather than produce photo-etch for a particular type of model, the sets from Voyager Model present equipment and fittings found on warships of the Imperial Japanese Navy. First produced in 2005, these sets feature relief-etching.

IJN Catapults AP-040

Included in the Voyager IJN Catapult set are two stainless steel photo-etch frets and a bag of resin parts. Fret A is the larger and contains six relief-etched catapults. In fact relief-etching is used on every surface of the catapults, other than the bottom. You can count the raised rivets on the sides or feel the raised grid pattern of the catapult decking to see the level of detail on these parts. Each catapult is one-piece with the sides, top and bottom folding together. However, before you fold a catapult together, you had better make sure that you have attached the resin parts inside of the catapult frame because Voyager supplies the cylinders that were inside the catapult frame.

Although new to the industry, Voyager products are exceptionally well detailed. With this set of Japanese catapults, Voyager even includes resin cylinders found within the catapult frame

IJN Watertight Doors AP-044

This two-fret set has the larger stainless steel fret contains 146 doors, all with doors open. If you wish to have a door shut, simply close it like the real thing. Each door has the rim fitting and sill above the door. The relief-etched doors come in fourteen styles, each divided into right-hand and left-hand doors. Some doors have front and back sides that fold together. Some have rounded tops and others square tops. They all have dogs, hinges, handles and other detail relief-etched on their surfaces. The smaller of the two frets, again in stainless steel, contains a wide assortment of deck hatches and skylights.

Below: Voyager Models produces photo-etch sets for not only common Japanese Navy fittings, but also for some quite esoteric subjects. One such 'off the beaten path' subject is this set of relief-etched emergency rudders with a smaller fret of life ring frames.

IJN Emergency Set AP-045

This provides six emergency rudders in gleaming brass on fret A. Each of the six rudders has two parts: the exterior layer with the relief-etching and an interior layer. Each layer folds together, so the completed emergency rudder will be four layers of brass thick. The brass parts of both layers already have the eyebolts used to secure the rudder to the cables from the ship. This fret also has 24 life rings. Fret B is of stainless steel and provides 12 life ring racks in two styles of six each.

IJN Ladder Set #1 AP-046

This two-fret set has inclined ladders on one fret and vertical ladders on the other so you cover all of the bases. Of course each inclined ladder comes with handrails that fold upward over the treadway, but what is different about this Voyager Model set is, firstly, individual bendable treads. Even with the best photo-etch producers the individual treads of an inclined ladder are likely to resemble bars in 1:700 scale. With this set not all but a substantial number of the inclined ladders have treads that can be bent at an angle from the ladder structure. The second difference is tread pattern. The treads in this set actually have a grid pattern. You may have to see it under magnification but this level of detail is phenomenal in 1:700 scale.

IJN AA Guns AP-047

With AP-047 Voyager Model provides sixteen single 25mm guns, twelve twin 25mm and twelve triple 25mm guns. This set also comes with two photo-etch sets. The largest fret is composed of stainless steel and contains the bulk of the gun fittings. The smaller brass fret contains the base plates for the various guns. Each triple gun consists of five parts; the twin mount has four parts; and single guns consist of four or three parts. The difference with the single guns involves the number of square base plates provided. For the single 25mm guns Voyager provides sixteen sets of: barrel, mounting and small circular base; however, only ten square plates are provided. Almost every one of the 166 total parts provided on these two frets is relief-etched. For each type of AA gun the modeller will have to fold the photo-etched parts to get it in the proper form, so it will take some level of comfort with working in photo-etch.

Bottom right: For this set on IJN boat handling gear, the modeller receives almost every type of davit and boat cradle used by the IJN. Also included is a smaller fret with rudders, propellers and propeller shafts for the ship's boats.

IJN Boat Equipment AP-048

The set consists of two photo-etch sets, the larger in brass and the smaller in stainless steel, plus one page of instructions. The quality of the parts on both frets is excellent. The large brass fret contains about 60% davits, 30% boat chocks and 10% boat fittings. There are five styles of davits. Each davit is one piece but folds onto itself to add extra thickness and a three-dimensional quality. Rigging and pulleys are worked into each one-piece davit and almost every piece is relief-etched. These are the best davits available, although each davit will require precision to fold. The boat chocks come in three styles. Two styles are used to cradle the heavier boats with three chocks.

ALL VOYAGER SAMPLES:
COURTESY VOYAGER MODEL

IJN Aircraft Deck Rail and Turntables AP-049

With Voyager AP-049 you receive two frets, one brass and one stainless steel. The brass fret is the larger of the two. This fret is devoted mostly to the deck railing but also has some items for the turntables. There are two styles of railing in the set. Voyager provides five sets of railing (a total of ten rails) for each of the two styles of railing, as well as two templates on this fret for drilling locator holes for their brass railing. First you would have to remove any plastic cast on railing, then use the templates to drill locator hulls and finally attach the rails. For the turntables, the brass fret provides eight turntable bases, in which the turntable rests. Lastly there are 16 rails for the turntable decks. The stainless steel fret contains the eight turntable decks. Each of these is beautifully relief-etched with the intricate Japanese grid pattern.

White Ensign Models

Based in the United Kingdom, White Ensign Models is one of the Old Guard of photo-etch design and production. WEM is run by Caroline Snyder, John Snyder and Dave Carter and the brass photo-etch is designed by 'Mad Pete' Hall. However, they have products other than just photo-etch that should be of great interest for modellers of the *Myoko* and *Takao* class cruisers.

White Ensign Models IJN Anti-Aircraft Weapons in 1:700 Scale, Set WEM PE728

No matter which 1:700 cruiser kit is purchased, this brass photo-etch fret from White Ensign Models will be very beneficial. As only the Skywave *Takao* class kits contain single 25mm AA guns in the part mix, what will the modeller do to replicate these for the Hasegawa *Myoko* class kits or the Aoshima *Takao* class kits? The solution is certainly this fret. This one fret includes: eleven Type 96 single 25mm guns, twenty Type 96 twin 25mm guns, twenty Type 96 triple 25mm guns, ten Lewis machine guns, eleven Type 93 twin 13mm machine guns and six Vickers single 40mm guns. The single 25mm guns and the Lewis machine guns will be easy to use but the multiple barrel guns require folding the brass to achieve the proper shape and have the reputation of being fiddly to assemble.

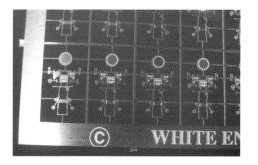

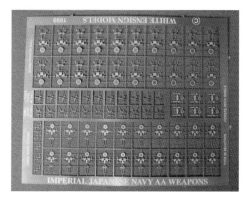

These are brass photo-etched triple 25mm AA guns found in the White Ensign Models fret of Imperial Japanese AA guns. Notice the high level of relief-etching found on these very small parts. These parts can be very fiddly in folding and assembling but are of unparalleled detail.

White Ensign Models IJN Doors and Hatches in 1:700 Scale, Set WEM PE729

This White Ensign Models product features 91 doors and 13 hatches in stainless steel. The doors come in four IJN styles with 13 doors per style. Two styles have rounded tops, one style has a square top and porthole and the other style has a square top with no window. Even in the newer kits the doors are missing or lack detail, so these photo-etch doors will add an extra measure of detail. White Ensign Models also produces a set of IJN Doors and Hatches in 1:350 Scale, WEM PE3518 but until kits of the *Myoko* or *Takao* classes appear in this scale, these are only useful on other models. These doors are larger brass cousins of the 1:700 scale set with the same mix of doors and hatches as found in the smaller set.

White Ensign Models Colourcoats Paints

As with every other navy, the Imperial Japanese Navy used its own paint formulas for their warships. There were four main yards employed by the IJN, located at Sasebo, Kure, Maizuru, and Yokosuka. Each yard used its own peculiar shade of grey paint for ships that were built or refitted in that yard. The colour of a particular cruiser depended upon the date of the last fit or yard repair. If a ship was refitted in a particular yard, she was repainted in that yard's colour. White Ensign Models produces a line of paints specifically formulated to match the tonal qualities of paints used by the Imperial Japanese Navy during World War Two. In the IJN Colourcoat line are found: Kure Grey, Maizuru Grey, Sasebo Grey, Yokosuka Grey, Deck Linoleum Brown, and Japanese Deck Tan. Also, various Japanese greens, used for late war carrier camouflage, are found in the Colourcoat IJN line.

The White Ensign Models Colourcoat range of paints is exactingly matched to the colour and tonal qualities of the paints used by the four major Japanese ship yards for the Imperial Japanese Navy. The monograph database *Imperial Japanese Navy Greys* by John Snyder provides an invaluable reference for the modeller who wishes to paint their model in the exact colours worn by the ship being modelled in the exact time frame.

White Ensign Models *Imperial Japanese Navy Greys, A Ship-By-Ship Compilation*

So how do you know what colour to paint your model cruiser? Well that depends upon her last stop at one of the four major Japanese yards. Of the four *Myoko* class cruisers, *Haguro* wore Sasebo and Kure grey at different times and the other three wore Sasebo, Kure, and Yokosuka grey at various times in their careers. A slightly less complex situation existed for the *Takao* class ships, but even here *Atago* wore Kure, Maizuru and Yokosuka grey during her career. With this pamphlet from White Ensign Models, the modeller can easily determine which shade of grey to use. The five-page data base reflects the times that each ship went through the different yards. Coverage includes carriers through torpedo boats. As an example, the *Chokai* would be painted in Yokosuka grey for the Battle of Savo Island, as she had been through the Yokosuka Yard in May 1942. Yet for the Battle of Leyte Gulf, the *Chokai* would be in Kure grey, as she had worn that colour since July 1944.

Takao and *Myoko* class models Currently in Production

Manufacturer, Ship and Kit Number	Remarks

1:200 Scale

Konishi *Takao/Atago* Class Konishi 31	Priced at 243,000 yen, this is the most detailed kit available
Konishi *Myoko* Konishi 35	Priced at 243,000 yen, this is the most detailed kit available

1:500 Scale

Konishi *Myoko* Konishi 5013	Priced at 27,000 yen
Konishi *Takao/Atago* Konishi 5031	Priced at 27,000 yen
Konishi *Chokai* Konishi 5032	Priced at 27,000 yen
Konishi *Maya* 1944 Konishi 5033	Priced at 27,000 yen
Nichimo IJN *Nachi* NI5001	Good, Reasonably priced kit.
Nichimo IJN *Haguro* NI5002	Good, Reasonably priced kit.
Nichimo IJN *Myoko* NI5003	Good, Reasonably priced kit.
Nichimo IJN *Ashigara* NI5004	Good, Reasonably priced kit.
Nichimo IJN *Atago* NIU5003	Poor kit but only affordable large scale kit of class
Nichimo IJN *Takao* NIU 5004	Poor kit but only affordable large scale kit of class
Nichimo IJN *Chokai* NIU5005	Poor kit but only affordable large scale kit of class
Nichimo IJN *Maya* NIU5006	Poor kit but only affordable large scale kit of class

1:700 Scale

Aoshima IJN *Takao* 1944 new tooling AOS00337

Aoshima IJN *Atago* 1942 new tooling AOS00338

Aoshima IJN *Maya* – Battle of Marianas 1944 new tooling AOS 00339

Aoshima IJN *Chokai* –1942 Battle of Solomon Islands new tooling AOS00340

Aoshima IJN *Maya* with Photo-Etch (new Tooling) AOS31025

Hasegawa IJN *Myoko* HAS43333

Hasegawa IJN *Nachi* HAS43334

Hasegawa IJN *Haguro* HAS43335

Hasegawa IJN *Ashigara* HAS43336

Skywave IJN *Takao* 1942 SWW54

Skywave IJN *Atago* 1941 SWW55

Skywave IJN *Takao* 1944 SWW57

Skywave IJN *Maya* 1944 SWW58

Skywave IJN *Chokai* 1944 SWW59

1:1200 Scale

Superior *Atago* 1944 J302

Superior *Chokai* 1944 J303

Superior *Nachi* J307

1:1250 Scale

Konishi *Myoko* Konishi 301

Konishi *Takao* Konishi 305

Konishi *Maya* 1944 Konishi 307

Konishi *Chokai* Konishi 308

Konishi *Haguro* 1929 Konishi 314

Neptun *Atago* 1944 N1232

Neptun *Maya* 1944 N1232a

Neptun *Chokai* 1944 N1232b

Neptun *Nachi* 1940 N1233

1:2400 Scale

GHQ *Maya* 1941 IJN11

GHQ *Myoko* IJN36

GHQ *Chokai* IJN45

Older Japanese Market Kits now out of production

Here's a list of vintage *Takao* and *Myoko* class kits. This data is taken from the 7th Edition of *The Collector's Value Guide for Scale Model Plastic Kits* by John W. Burns: Courtesy of Jeff Herne

ASK, Japan. These kits appeared in the 1960s with a few re-issued later by Saito. Some of these were also re-packaged in and re-issued in the early 1970s by Balboa

Kit No. 21 *Nachi/Haguro* 1/1000 scale

Kit No. 23 *Myoko/Ashigara* 1/1000 scale

Kit No. 25 *Maya* 1/1000 scale

Kit No. 26 *Atago* 1/1000 scale

Kit No. 27 *Takao* 1/1000 scale

Bandai, Japan. These kits ended production in 1985.

Kit No. 8408 *Myoko*, 1/550 scale

Kit. No. 8409 *Atago*, 1/550 scale

Kit No. 8410 *Chokai* 1/550 scale

Bandai also released 1/2000 scale kits:

Kit No. 7 *Myoko* (with I-16 sub)

Kit No. 8 *Takao* (with I-1 sub)

BMW, UK. This was a mail-order retail shop in the UK which closed in the early 1980s. In 1967-68 several ship kits were issued under the 'Green Label' series.

Kit No. GL-7 *Myoko*, 1/400 scale (ex-Tamiya)

Kit No. GL-8 *Haguro*, 1/400 scale (ex-Tamiya)

Doyusha, Japan

Kit. No. 11 *Haguro*, 1/700 scale

They also released kits later on with no numbers:

Atago, 1/700 scale

Myoko, 1/700 scale

Imai, Japan. Ship production ended in 1985.

Maya, 1/550 scale

Ashigara, 1/550 scale

Marusan, Japan. One of the first plastic kit companies in Japan, Marusan also released the first-ever kit of the SSN *Nautilus*, issued in 1954. The company went out of business in the early 1970s.

Kit No. 509 *Chokai*, 1/700 scale

Kit No. 530 *Myoko*, 1/700 scale

Nippon Hobby, Japan. Sometimes called Nihon Hobby.

Haguro, 1/1000 scale

Paramount, USA. This company reboxed and re-issued kits from several Japanese manufacturers.

Kit No. 212 *Chokai*, 1/550 scale (most likely ex-Bandai)

Saito, Japan. These kits appeared in the late 1960s and were from the ASK moulds. Some of these were also re-packaged in and re-issued in the early 1970s by Balboa.

Kit No. 3 *Chokai/Takao* 1/1000 scale

Kit No. 4 *Maya* 1/1000 scale

Kit No. 5 *Atago* 1/1000 scale

Kit No. 6 *Takao* 1/1000 scale

Tamiya, Japan. These kits were available in the 1980s but have not been seen for some time.

Kit No. 3 *Myoko*, 1/400 scale

Kit No. 4 *Haguro*, 1/400 scale

Kit No. JD-005 *Chokai*, 1/400 scale

Modelmakers' Showcase

Skywave Maya 1944 by Claudio Matteini

Italian modeller Claudio Matteini decided to build the IJN heavy cruiser *Maya* because she was the only cruiser of the *Takao* class to be converted to an AA cruiser. The model depicts the *Maya* on 17 October 1944, at Lingga Roads, just a few days before being sunk on the 23rd by four torpedoes launched by US submarine *Dace* in the Palawan Passage, north of Borneo, while *Maya* was underway to Philippines with Vice Admiral Kurita's fleet. The kit is the 1:700 scale Skywave version and he improved the model with a lot of scratch-building and great deal of photo-etched parts. It is quite impossible to show how much scratch-building was involved during the construction of the *Maya*. The original Skywave kit is composed of about 200 plastic parts but at the end of the work, more than 3,500 parts went into the model. Claudio used photo-etched parts from Tom's Modelworks, Gold Medal Models, Fine Molds, Joe World, White Ensign Models, Hasegawa and Pit Road, together with metal sets from Pit Road for 203mm gun barrels and Clipper Models for

127mm gun barrels and different sizes of mushroom vents. For all of the photo-etch parts not readily available in sets, Claudio worked and adapted other photo-etch parts. The tripod mainmast is made of metal rods of different sizes and rigging is obtained by stretching plastic sprue. The tower bridge structure, funnels, central structure around the funnels with its 25mm triple machine guns, the aft structure under the tripod mainmast, 203mm gun turrets and rangefinders, 127mm AA guns, aircraft deck and all the details on the main deck were heavily improved or scratch-built. The Aichi E13A1 'Jake' Navy type O reconnaissance floatplane is scratch-built and the canopy is open. *Maya* was airbrushed with White Ensign Models Colourcoat WEM CC04: IJN Yokosuka Grey, referring to Snyder & Short Enterprises information contained in their *Imperial Japanese Navy World War II Ship Colours*, and softly dry-brushed with three different shades of grey. The linoleum decks were painted with WEMCC10: IJN linoleum, and dry-brushed with light brown and yellow.

It is hard to believe that this replica of *Maya* is in 1:700 scale but it is. Italian modeller, Claudio Matteini, used over 3,500 parts to represent the *Maya* on 17 October 1944 at Linga Roads before sailing for Leyte Gulf.

At the lower left corner is seen the type of accommodation ladder used by the IJN. They would frequently have a canvas shelter over a metal frame at the top of the ladder.

With this overhead view, it is easy to see how the booms at the stern with their suspended boarding ladders were used. A boat would pull under the boom and crewmen would use the rope ladders to embark or leave the ship.

The use of brown linoleum panels secured by brass strips was unique to Japanese cruisers and destroyers. Models of these ships will certainly contrast with those replicating wood planked or metal decks.

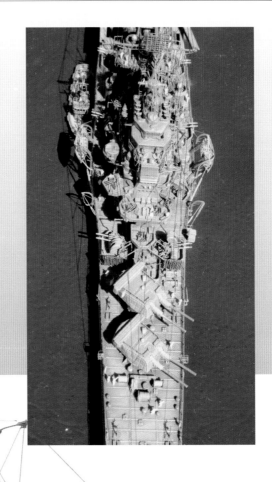

In another photograph which reflects the additional AA mounts fitted in lieu of C turret, the extra deckhouse with triple 25mm mounts and twin 127mm DP mounts are clearly seen. The new guns, plus the two triple 25mm guns mounted on sponsons just aft of the new additions provided for a very heavy concentration of AA fire forward.

Notice that Mr. Matteini has even added fenders for the tug boat in this photograph of the starboard side in his greatly enhanced build of the Skwave 1944 *Maya* kit.

Even in 1:700 scale, the massive bridge of the *Takao* class cruisers makes it the classic signature of the class.

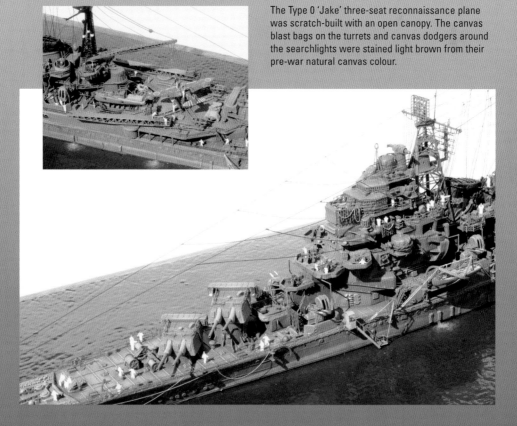

The Type 0 'Jake' three-seat reconnaissance plane was scratch-built with an open canopy. The canvas blast bags on the turrets and canvas dodgers around the searchlights were stained light brown from their pre-war natural canvas colour.

For the AA conversion C or No 3 turret of *Maya* was removed and in its place a deckhouse with three 25mm mounts, flanked by two twin 127mm DP mounts was installed.

Skywave *Takao 1944* by George Hargreaves

This is the Imperial Japanese Navy heavy cruiser *Takao*. She is depicted launching a first reconnaissance for operation SHO GO, destined for the San Bernardino Strait. USS *Darter* ended *Takao's* participation and operation SHO GO became known as the Battle of Leyte Gulf. This is the 1:700 scale Skywave kit, with Gold Medal Models IJN Cruiser brass, White Ensign Models 25mm brass, Pit Road crew brass and other bits. Paint is WEM Colourcoats.

IJN TAKAO

Mr. Hargreaves added a great deal of visual interest by included a large number of crew figures in animated positions. Their white uniforms starkly contrast with the dark metal decks and deck linoleum.

With upward slanting yardarms, the tripod foremast, which replaced the quadruped foremast in the 1939 refit of *Takao* and *Atago*, always distinguished that pair from *Chokai* and *Maya*, which retained the quadruped mast. The Type 22 radar is seen at the top of the foremast.

The mainmast of *Takao* and *Atago* were moved 70 feet aft to just forward of X (No 4) barbette during their 1939 refit. Throughout their careers, *Takao* and *Atago* were almost identical in appearance. *Chokai* and *Maya* took on very different forms.

Shown on the flight deck and catapults are two Type 0 'Pete', two-seat tactical reconnaissance floatplanes and one Type 0 'Jake' three-seat long-range reconnaissance aircraft. This was the ideal complement in 1942 and 1943, but by 1944 the typical aircraft complement was two Type 0 'Jakes'. The long range of the three-place aircraft was now far more important than the shell-spotting of the tactical two-seat aircraft.

This is the Skywave *Takao* 1944 by George Hargreaves. She is depicted launching a first reconnaissance for operation SHO GO, destined for the San Bernardino Strait.

Schemes *Drawn by George Richardson*

MYOKO 1941 *Overall grey*

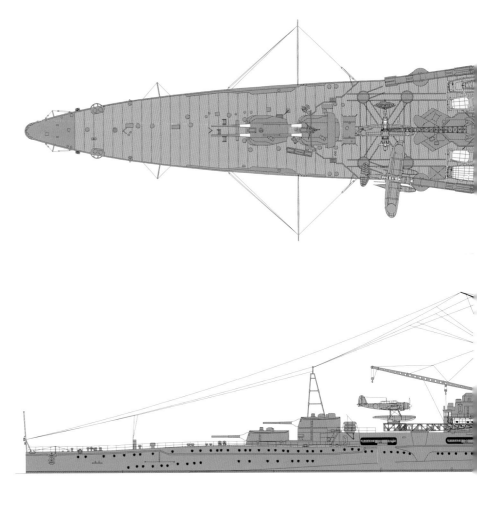

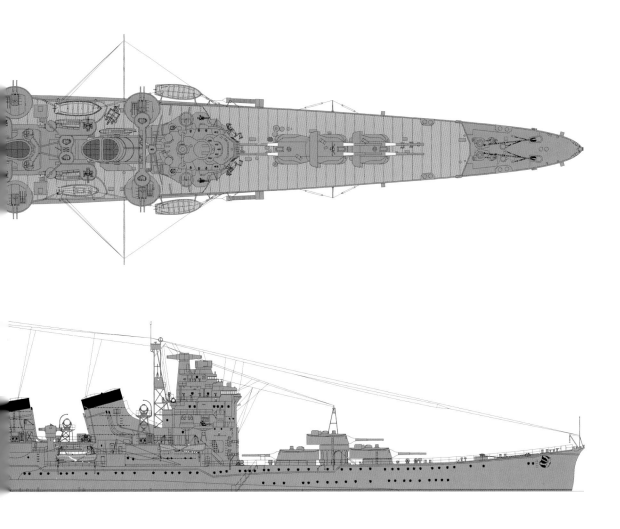

MYOKO 1945 *Reconstruction of camouflage scheme*

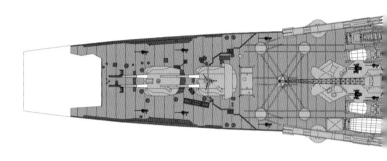

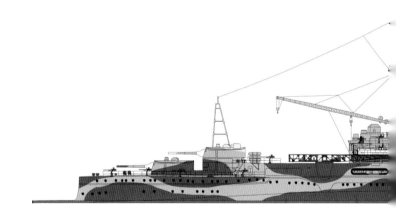

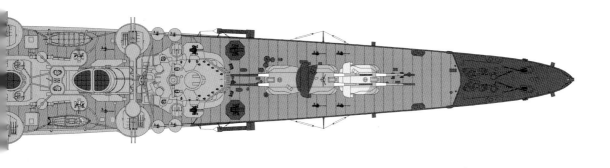

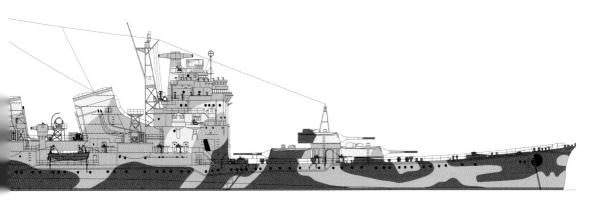

Hasegawa *Nachi* by Bob Cicconi

Here are some photographs of Hasegawa's re-tooled 1:700 scale Japanese heavy cruiser *Nachi* that was built by Bob Cicconi. The ship is shown after its second rebuild in 1941, as she would have appeared at the Battle of Java Sea early in 1942. Hasegawa also gives you the option of building it in its final form with extra AA and slightly different masts and aerials. The model seems to be just about right-on according to Lacroix's book on Japanese heavy cruisers in World War Two. Although the kit is redone, Hasegawa still had moulded steps on the main deck. Bob removed all six steps and replaced them with photo-

etched units. He used Tom's Modelworks IJN Heavy Cruiser photo-etch kit, and also Gold Medal Model's Ultra IJN railings. At first Bob was nervous about using them, but although they are petite, they are no more difficult to use than other photo-etch railings. In addition, they are a necessity when doing the Japanese ships, which have an upward bow curve/sheer forward of the superstructure. He also dry brushed it and used a watercolour wash, stretched sprue aerials and Celluclay for the water. Bob used White Ensign Model's paints for the grey and linoleum on the ship, and Extracolor IJN dark green and grey for the aircraft.

Nachi would have been fitted with the ideal complement of two two-seat reconnaissance floatplanes and one three-seat long-range floatplane. However, in March 1942 the Type 94 'Alf' was still in service, rather than the Type 0 'Jake' and the Type 95 'Dave' would have been the two-seat floatplanes, rather than the Type 0 'Pete'. The 'Jake' and 'Pete' did not come into service until late 1942.

All photographs by Robert Doebley.

This model was built almost right from the box. The biggest exception is the use of photo-etch, which provides a far better appearance than the comparable plastic part. The photo-etch towers, crane and catapult shown in this photograph emphasise the desirability of using photo-etch.

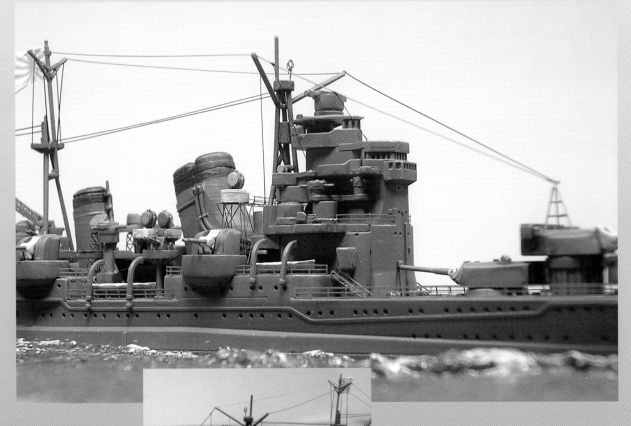

The torpedo bulges, expanded in the 1939-1940 refit are clearly shown here. Canvas dodgers and blast bags are still shown in natural canvas colour. Photographic evidence tends to suggest that the IJN adopted staining these canvas items light brown in 1941

Photo-etch can provide many things for the 1:700 scale kits of the *Myoko* and *Takao* class cruisers. However, there is no new photo-etch products devoted solely to either class of cruisers. The new kits may be far improved over the 1972 kits but some parts are still too heavy. Both masts, but especially the foremast, are too heavy in plastic. Photo-etch brass replacements are desperately needed. Hopefully some photo-etch producer will awake to the fact that a specialised fret tailored to each class would have a significant market. Presently there are ten 1:700 kits of the *Takao* class in production, which provides a ready market for a fret tailored for that class.

This is the Hasegawa *Nachi* 1942 (New Tooled) by Bob Cicconi and photographed by Bob Doebley. Mr. Cicconi decided to portray *Nachi* in her appearance at the Battle of the Java Sea in March 1942.

In March 1942 the *Nachi* still presented a somewhat narrow and very clean bridge. Only *Myoko* had received wind baffles at this point. In 1943 the class would change appreciably in appearance. The First Wartime Modernisation in early 1943 would expand the width of the bridge to add AA control to the top deck, baffles to the bridge face and add Type 22 radar. The Second Wartime Modernisation in late 1943 would dramatically expand the numbers of 25mm AA guns carried by the class.

This photograph also emphasises the fine appearance made with the addition of photo-etch parts to replace solid plastic parts provided in the kit. The open iron-work of the catapults, crane, searchlight towers and aircraft trolleys cannot be duplicated using solid plastic parts.

Nichimo *Myoko* in 1:500 Scale by Jeff Herne

The Nichimo models of the *Myoko* class are the most affordable kit of the class in a scale larger than 1:700. The Nichimo *Myoko* model is greatly superior to that company's models of the *Takao* class ships, also in 1:500 scale. Although it is an older kit, it is still amenable to completion as a very attractive replica without major surgery. The *Myoko* is portrayed after her Second Wartime Modernisation from November to December 1943. This is indicated by the single 25mm guns on the forecastle and quarterdeck. The 25mm guns do not come with the Nichimo kit and were scratch-built. Brass photo-etch fittings in 1:500 scale from Tom's Modelworks were used throughout the build.

Myoko Class Heavy Cruiser IJN Nachi 1944

The Nichimo kit was designed as an early-war version of the ship. In 1944 the *Myoko* would have been fitted with a wider upper bridge level for AA control and wind baffles for the bridge face.

This is the Nichimo *Myoko* in 1:500 Scale by Jeff Herne. The Nichimo models of the *Myoko* class are the most affordable kit of the class in a scale larger than 1:700 and there is a significant jump in size between 1:700 and 1:500 scale.

Below: By 1944 the standard aircraft complement of the class was two Type 0 'Jake' three-seat long range reconnaissance aircraft, as shown in this model.

Appearance

This is *Ashigara* in 1937 or 1938. She has received her First Modernisation completed by 1936 but not her Second Modernisation started in 1939. She carries a E8N2 Type 95 'Dave' two-seat tactical reconnaissance floatplane on each catapult. The aircraft entered service in December 1936.

MYOKO CLASS

This class was subject to almost continuous alteration, so only an outline can be given here. Soon after completion the forward funnels were raised by 2m to keep stack fumes from the bridge (1931-2) and special funnel caps were added.

The London Naval Treaty left Japan with no additional cruiser tonnage available, so, the Japanese Admiralty immediately began to consider upgrading existing ships, the four *Myoko*s being given priority.

FIRST MODERNISATION (SASEBO NOVEMBER 1934 TO JUNE 1936

The main features are summarised in the table, but it is worth mentioning that the torpedo tubes were placed on the upper deck inside sponsons that were to be outboard from the hull to give some protection from the explosion of their own warheads. A new shelter deck was added aft of the funnels, the hangar deleted, and a rail system adopted to spot the four scout planes for operations. Additional bulges would be placed atop the original underwater

bulges, which slightly increased the waterline beam. Together, all of the changes added 680 tons to displacement.

These changes were only the first step in the modernisation of the class, some minor changes being made later at Sasebo: searchlights relocated to towers abreast both funnels; HA directors moved to the bridge in the original searchlight positions, and quadruple 13.2mm Hotchkiss machine guns mounted in their place either side

This is *Ashigara* at Portsmouth in May 1937 for the Coronation Review of King George VI. She is fresh from her First Modernisation. This photograph reflects the changes in this refit with twin 127mm secondary guns replacing the original single 120mm mounts. Also seen is the upper, above waterline torpedo blister added atop the original torpedo bulge. This blister would be further increased in her Second Modernisation in 1939.

of the fore funnel; and the two 7.7mm Lewis guns moved from either side of the aft funnel to sponsons on either side of the middle bridge. A third step addressed the structural weakness revealed by damage to *Myoko* during a typhoon in September 1935 by riveting steel on either side of the keel and also below the upper deck (January to March 1936). A fourth step added a heavier derrick and strengthened the tripod mainmast in order to handle heavier floatplanes (May to June 1936).

Two years later plans for a more radical Second Modernisation were completed (June 1938) but the program had to wait until slots were available in the over-worked yards. Reconstruction orders for *Nachi* and *Haguro* were issued in January 1939 and for *Ashigara* and *Myoko* in April 1939, the work being carried out as follows: *Haguro* (to December 1939); *Nachi* (to March 1940); *Ashigara* (June 1939 to June 1940); and lastly *Myoko* (March 1940 to April 1941).

SECOND MODERNISATION

Again, readers are referred to the summary table, but the reconstruction also involved removing the upper level of the bridge, producing a lower and lighter tower. Additionally, the *Myoko*, which refitted last, was a test bed for the fitting of wind baffles to the forward edge of the bridge at the compass level. The pole foremast was replaced with a tripod, and besides the light AA in the table, two Type 93 13mm machine guns were added in bridge sponsons. The two additional quadruple 610mm torpedo mounts were added to the forward end of the deck sponson. Planned aircraft complement was one Type 0 'Jake' three-seat plane for long distance reconnaissance (starboard catapult) and two Type 0 'Pete' two-seaters for shell-splash spotting and battlefield reconnaissance (one on port catapult and one on a trolley). The new aircraft were not available and it was not until November 1941 that the *Myoko* class had a uniform complement of one 'Jake'

Above: This is *Myoko* in September 1937 after her First Modernisation. In this refit from 1935 to 1936 *Myoko* was given an upper torpedo bulge, as seen in this photograph, to improve her stability from her overweight construction.

Below: A Second Modernisation in 1939 further changed her appearance by reducing the height of the upper bridge levels, increasing the size of the upper torpedo bulge and adding a second torpedo mount in each sponson.

Gun Characteristics					
Ordnance	Purpose	Range	Vertical range	Rate of fire rpm	Shell weight
200mm/50 (7.9in)	Surface	26.700m	NA	4-5 max / 2-3 norm	110 kg
203mm/50 (8in)	DP	29,400m	12,000m	4-5 max / 2-3 norm	123.85 kg
120mm/45 HA	DP	15,600m	10,065m	10-11 max	20.45 kg
127mm/40 HA	DP	14,800m	9,400m	14 max / 11-12 norm	23.45 kg
40mm/62	AA	13,000m	7,000m	200 max / 100 norm	2.2 kg
25mm/60	AA	7,500m	5,250m	260 max / 115 norm	.24 to .26 kg
13mm/76	AA	6,500m	4,500m	475 max / 250 norm	.04 to .05 kg
7.7mm	AA	4,000m	3,000m	550 max	.01 kg

Opposite: Wartime photographs of the class are rare. This is *Nachi* on 20 September 1943 and shows her after her First Wartime Modification. In this her AA complement was increased. The two bridge 13mm guns were replaced by twin 25mm mounts. Two Type 96 twin 25mm mounts were added abreast of the mainmast. The AA command level of the upper bridge was enlarged and baffles added to front edge as fitted on *Myoko* in 1941. The bridge baffles and enlarged upper bridge are very evident in this photograph.

Taken in May 1941, this photograph shows *Nachi* after her Second Modernisation. There is a new deck rail pattern for aircraft handling and tripod foremast. The enlarged torpedo blisters can be seen, even from this overhead angle.

and two Type 94 'Dave' two-seat planes.

These additions increased displacement by 400 tons, and larger torpedo bulges replaced those fitted during the First Modernisation. Beam increased by 1.73m. Watertight steel tubes were added to the void of the new upper bulge and original lower bulge. Upon completion the trial displacement of the cruisers was 14,900 metric tons.

After 7 December 1941 there was little time for further extensive refits, but there were limited improvements.

WARTIME MODIFICATIONS
The first (April to September 1943) enlarged the AA command level of the upper bridge and added baffles to front edge as fitted on *Myoko* in 1941. The two bridge 13mm guns were replaced by twin 25mm mounts, and two more twin 25mm were added abreast of the mainmast. Type 21 mattress radar was fitted to the foremast with the radar room inside the tripod. The loss of carriers required additional long-range reconnaissance assets, so the new complement, except for *Nachi*, was two 'Jakes' and one 'Pete', but by 1944 the complement was just the two 'Jakes'.

The second (1943-1944) added eight single 25mm guns to all, and Type 22 radar to *Nachi* and *Ashigara*. These additions were made to *Myoko* and *Haguro* in November–December 1943, for *Nachi* November 1943 to January 1944 and for *Ashigara* in March 1944. A third alteration (1944) added extra

Summary of Modifications to Myoko Class

Main armament	Secondary	Light AA	Torpedo tubes	Other changes
As Completed 1929				
Ten 200mm (7.9in) 5 x 2	Six 120mm (4.7in) 6 x 1	Two 7.7mm MG	Twelve 61cm 4 x 3 fixed	Torpedo bulge entirely below waterline; one catapult; two aircraft
First Modernisation 1934-1936				
	Eight 127mm (5in) 4 x 2	Two 13mm MG Two 7.7mm MG	Eight 61cm 2 x 4 trainable	Additional torpedo bulge placed atop original; two catapults; four 'Dave' (2-seat) aircraft
Second Modernisation 1939-1941				
Ten 203mm (8in) 5 x 2		Eight 25mm 4 x 2	Sixteen 61cm 4 x 4 trainable	Rebuilt, lower bridge; upper bulge enlarged; one 'Jake' (3-seat), two 'Pete' (2-seat) aircraft
First Wartime Modification 1943				
		Sixteen 25mm 8 x 2		Type 21 radar; two 'Jake' (3-seat), one 'Pete' (2-seat) aircraft
Second Wartime Modification 1943-44				
		Twenty-four 25mm 8 x 2 & 8 x 1		Type 22 radar in *Nachi* and *Ashigara*; lower row of hull scuttles plated over
Third Wartime Modification 1944				
		25mm: Fifty-two in *Myoko* and *Haguro*; forty-eight in *Ashigara*; forty-two in *Nachi*		Type 22 radar in *Myoko* and *Haguro*; two 'Jake' (3-seat) aircraft

25mm guns to all, but the composition and location varied from ship to ship. *Myoko* and *Haguro* were fitted in June 1944 with an extra four triple 25mm mounts, two on the quarterdeck and two between the bridge and No 3 turret, and sixteen single 25mm guns. These two also received their Type 22 radar at this time. *Nachi* and *Ashigara* were modified in September 1944 and received an additional two twin 25mm, between the bridge and No 3 turret, and twenty single 25mm guns.

Throughout the war the *Myoko* class cruisers were painted a single colour grey, the exact shade being determined by the last Navy Yard which had worked on the ship, Kure, Sasebo, Yokosuka and Maizuru each having its own. However, after *Myoko* became an immobile AA platform at Singapore in 1944, she received a two-tone camouflage of dark grey splotches over a medium grey base, while *Nachi* had her aft funnel painted white for operations in the Aleutian Islands in 1943. Unlike other navies, the Imperial Japanese Navy did not use boot-topping, so the lower hull anti-fouling red would start where the upper grey ended. The Japanese anti-fouling lower hull red had a distinctive brown tinge to it.

This is *Takao* on 20 May 1932 shortly before she was commissioned. Clearly shown is the alternative solution adopted in this class to the inboard fixed hull torpedo mounts of the *Myoko* class. By placing the quadruple torpedo mounts in sponsons outside of the hull interior, accidental detonation of a warhead would reduce damage to the ship. This solution was worked into the *Myoko* class in their First Modernisation. *Takao* and *Chokai* had four square ports aft of the first torpedo mount while *Atago* and *Maya* had only three such ports.

Right: Taken in March 1932 during the trials of *Takao*, this photograph displays the multiple levels to the design's upper bridge. The light tripod in the foreground is a stanchion for a deck awning.

Below: The light quadruped foremast and heavy tower bridge of *Takao* are evident in this photograph taken on 23 May 1932, eight days before the cruiser was commissioned. The degree to which the torpedo deck sponsons overhung the hull is also well shown.

TAKAO CLASS

Since the cruisers of the *Takao* class were newer than the *Myoko*s, they received very few alterations early in their careers. In August 1933 new HA directors were installed. As a result of the typhoon damage to *Myoko* in September 1935, the *Takao* class also received hull strengthening plates from May to September 1936, *Takao* and *Maya* also received heavier lattice cranes to the mainmast for aircraft handling, to replace the pole derricks originally fitted. In *Maya* blast screens for the searchlight towers were removed and new searchlights fitted. Further

Right: This photograph from the bridge of *Maya* exhibits two features of Japanese cruisers. The deck covering was composed of panels of brown linoleum running across the width of the deck. The panels were secured to each other by thin brass strips screwed into the deck. During peacetime these brass strips were highly polished but during the war they were allowed to tarnish or painted grey. Also shown is a good profile of the blast bags. Left natural canvas in colour before the war, they were stained to a light brown during the war.

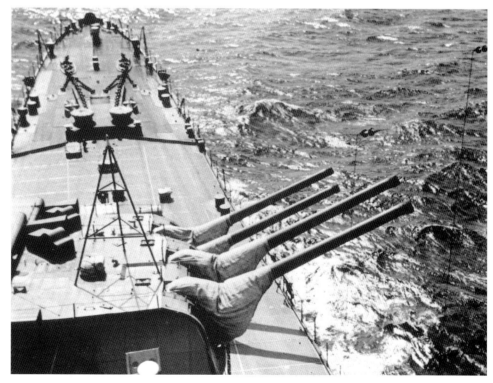

minor modifications were made in 1937 and 1938. In May-June 1937 *Takao* received the new searchlights, a shortened foremast and added a radar room inside the quadruped foremast. From October 1936 to July 1937 *Chokai* received the same treatment, as well as replacement of the Vickers 40mm guns by quadruple Hotchkiss 13.2mm guns and the new lattice crane. *Maya* received the radar room and AA replacement in December 1937 to January 1938. Other than hull strengthening plates, *Atago* did not receive these modifications.

By 1937 plans were underway to thoroughly modernise the *Takao* class, scheduled from 1938 to 1939 for *Takao* and *Atago*, with *Chokai* and *Maya* to follow in 1940 to 1941. *Takao* underwent modernisation from May 1938 to August 1939 and *Atago* from April 1938 to October 1939, but war intervened before *Maya* or *Chokai* could be taken in hand. Thereafter ships of the *Takao* class could be easily identified as to which group they belonged.

On 1 May 1938 *Takao* was at Yokosuka awaiting her Modernisation. This photograph shows her appearance on that day with RDF shack mounted inside the quadruped foremast and totally inadequate 7.7mm machine gun abreast of the forward funnel.

In another photograph from 1 May 1938 the aft amidships section of *Takao* is shown. A Vickers 40mm AA mount can be seen abreast of the aft funnel. This was replaced by a twin 25mm mount during Modernisation. Note the open deck behind the catapult and mainmast aft of the rear funnel. Other features of the Modernisation of *Takao* and *Atago* were the move of the mainmast to just forward of No 4 barbette and the shelter deck was extended to that barbette.

On 14 July 1939 *Takao* ran full power trials after her Modernisation refit. Even with the addition of an upper torpedo blister to improve stability and lessen draft, the wake would still swamp the lower row of scuttles if they were open. Her new tripod foremast and relocation of her mainmast to just forward of No 4 barbette are clearly shown. During these trials *Takao* hit 34.25 knots at 133,100shp on the measured mile.

FIRST MODERNISATION (*TAKAO* AND *ATAGO* 1938-1939)

The main details are given in the summary table. The four Type 96 twin 25mm guns were positioned on either side of both funnels and the two Type 93 twin 13mm on bridge sponsons (replaced by twin 25mm mounts in the fall of 1941). New gun platforms for the planned twin 127mm (5in) were added but the new guns were not actually installed until March and April 1942 in unshielded mounts. Two four-charge depth charge racks were added to the stern. The upper bridge was rebuilt to reduce topweight and received new range finders. The aircraft deck rails were changed to match the pattern already installed on the *Myoko* class, along with the heavier catapults. After the refit one Type 94 'Alf' three-seat and two Type 95 'Dave' two-seat floatplanes were carried, but the Type 0 'Jake' replaced the 'Alf' in November 1942 and the Type 0 'Pete' replaced the 'Dave' in 1942.

The torpedo bulge was enlarged along the same lines as those in the modernised *Myoko* class, so *Takao* and *Atago* had torpedo bulges that were visible above the waterline while *Maya* and *Chokai* did not. The new torpedo bulges greatly increased stability: revised design draft was 6.41m but at trial displacement of 14,838 metric tons, the draft was 6.32m. New bilge keels were also fitted.

When it was clear that *Maya* and *Chokai* could not receive the same modernisation, a few less extensive changes were made in 1941. The twin torpedo mounts were adapted to receive the newest model of 610mm torpedo. The new heavier catapults were also installed, although they initially received the same complement of floatplanes as *Takao* and *Atago*. The quadruple 13mm machine guns on either side of the aft funnel were replaced by Type 96 twin 25mm mounts and twin 13mm machine gun mounts were added on either side of the bridge.

After the Dutch East Indies operations, *Maya* and *Chokai* had the twin 13mm guns on the bridge replaced by twin 25mm guns and two additional twin 25mm mounts were placed on either side of the forward stack. They also received the two depth charge racks at the stern, as previously fitted to *Takao* and *Atago*. At the end of the Guadalcanal campaign, in February 1943 the *Takao* class was slated for their First Wartime Modification. *Takao* and *Atago* were refitted from July to August 1943 with additional light AA of two triple 25mm mounts on either side of the mainmast, Type 21 radar and bridge wind baffles. *Maya* and *Chokai* received two additional twin 25mm mounts on either side of the mainmast, Type 21 radar and wind baffles from August to September 1943.

The *Takao* class cruisers, less *Maya*, received their Second Wartime Modification in the same time period as

This is *Atago* on 25 August 1939 and clearly depicts the changes made to her during the Modernisation. The shelter deck has been extended from the rear stack to No 4 barbette and the mainmast has been moved 70 feet (25m) to the rear to just forward of that barbette. A tripod replaced the quadruped foremast and the upper bridge was reduced in height. Only *Atago* and *Takao* received this refit.

This is the massive bridge of *Takao* on 21 December 1939 after her Modernisation. Her upper bridge has been reduced in height and a tripod replaced the quadruped foremast. The new twin 25mm AA mount is shown abreast of the funnel and twin 13mm machine guns have been added to sponsons on either side of the bridge. Notice the 610mm torpedoes swung outboard. To reduce the threat to the ship by accidental explosion of one of their warheads, doctrine called for them to be swung outboard in this fashion before going into battle.

the ships of the *Myoko* class. *Atago* from November to December 1943 and *Takao* from November 1943 to January 1944 received the same treatment, but *Chokai*, at Truk, only had ten single 25mm guns added. *Maya*, however, received a unique refit: she was rebuilt as an anti-aircraft cruiser from December 1943 to April 1944 at Yokosuka. No 3 203mm gun turret and the existing AA armament was removed, and replaced by the new battery shown in the table. Her torpedo armament was also brought up to standard and a centreline depth charge rail added. She was equipped to handle two new Model 11 Zuiun floatplanes

but only carried two 'Jakes'. After these changes, standard displacement rose to 13,350 tons and trial to 15,159 tons. It was planned to give *Chokai* the same conversion as *Maya* but this plan was shelved.

By the summer of 1944 the four ships of the *Takao* class presented three distinctly different appearances, with *Takao* and *Atago* substantially identical, *Maya* unique in her AA configuration, and *Chokai* the only unit retaining her pre-war appearance with single 120mm mounts, twin torpedo tubes and no above-water torpedo bulge. The Third Wartime Modification for the *Takao* class was conducted in June and

Taken between May 1940 and May 1941 this photograph shows *Maya* as 4th Cruiser Squadron (Sentai) flagship. The *Takao* class cruisers were placed in the 4th Sentai before the war, while the *Myoko* class formed the 5th Sentai. Other than the old single 4.7in (120mm) heavy DP guns, her only AA defence was in the form of totally inadequate single Vickers 7.7mm machine guns abreast the forward funnel and quadruple Hotchkiss 13mm machine guns abreast the rear funnel.

This is *Chokai*, photographed in 1940. *Chokai* was originally slated to receive the same modernisation that was given to *Takao* and *Atago* in 1940 but the refit was cancelled in order to ready the fleet for war. As a consequence, the upper levels of the bridge retained their initial appearance in large measure. The horizontal yardarm on the foremast is another feature of the unmodernised *Chokai* and *Maya*; *Atago* and *Takao* after modernisation had yardarms which slanted upwards.

July 1944. *Takao* and *Atago* continued to be twins with each receiving an additional four triple and twenty-two single 25mm gun mounts. *Maya* received an additional eighteen single 25mm mounts. *Chokai* had the fewest changes, with twelve extra single mounts, as she did not have the additional stability conferred by enlarged torpedo bulges. This was the last appearance for the ships of the class, as *Atago*, *Maya* and *Chokai* were sunk during the Battle of Leyte Gulf. Although *Takao* managed to limp back to Singapore after being torpedoed in the Palawan passage, she was not repaired. She remained an immobile AA platform and survived the war. She was the last of the Japanese heavy cruisers, as she was not scuttled until 26 October 1946, almost four months after *Myoko*.

Summary of Modifications to Takao Class

Main armament	Secondary	Light AA	Torpedo tubes	Other changes
As Completed 1932				
Ten 203mm (8in) 5 x 2	Four 120mm (4.7in) 4 x 1	Two 40mm MG Two 7.7mm MG	Eight 61cm 4 x 2 trainable	Torpedo bulge entirely below waterline; two catapult; three aircraft
First Modernisation 1938-39 (Takao & Atago only)				
	Received eight 127mm (4 x 2) in 1942	Eight 25mm, 4 x 2 Four 13mm, 2 x 2	Sixteen 61cm 4 x 4 trainable	Additional torpedo bulge placed atop original; mainmast moved aft; bridge height reduced; tripod foremast replaced quadruped mast: one 'Alf' (3-seat), one 'Dave' (2-seat) aircraft; four depth charge racks
First Wartime Modification 1943 Atago & Takao				
		Eighteen 25mm 2 x 3 & 6 x 2		Type 21 radar
First Wartime Modification 1943 Maya & Chokai				
	As completed	Sixteen 25mm 8 x 2	As completed	Type 21 radar
Second Wartime Modification 1943-44 Atago & Takao				
		Twenty-six 25mm 2 x 3, 6 x 2 & 8 x 1		Type 22 radar; lower row of hull scuttles plated over
Second Wartime Modification 1943 Chokai				
	As completed	Twenty-six 25mm 8 x 2, 10 x 1	As completed	
AA Cruiser Refit 1943-44 Maya only (Chokai was also to receive this refit but it was not started)				
Eight 203mm (8in) 4 x 2	Twelve 127mm (5in) 6 x 2	Forty-eight 25mm 13 x 3, 9 x 1; thirty- six 13mm moveable mg; two 7.7mm mg	Sixteen 61cm 4 x 4 trainable	Additional torpedo bulge placed atop original; Type 22 radar; one depth charge rack; two 'Jake' (3-seat) aircraft
Third Wartime Modification 1944 Atago & Takao				
		Sixty 25mm 6 x 3, 6 x 2, 30 x 1		Type 13 radar
Third Wartime Modification 1944 Maya				
		Sixty-six 25mm 13 x 3, 27 x 1		Type 13 radar
Third Wartime Modification 1944 Chokai				
		Thirty-eight 25mm 8 x 2, 22 x 1		Type 13 radar (*Chokai* was the least modified of the class and the only one to keep the 120mm guns and twin torpedo mounts and not to increase the size of her torpedo bulge)

Plans *Drawn by George Richardson, 1:700 scale*

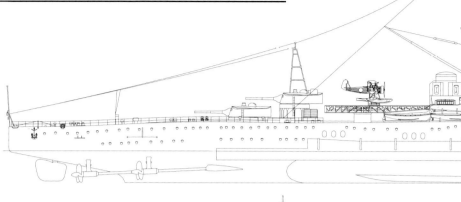

Myoko 1930
Plan & Profile

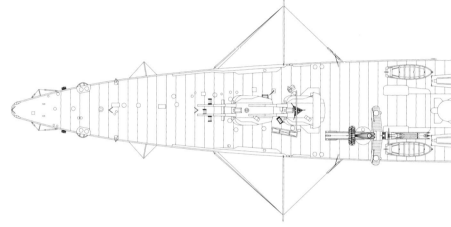

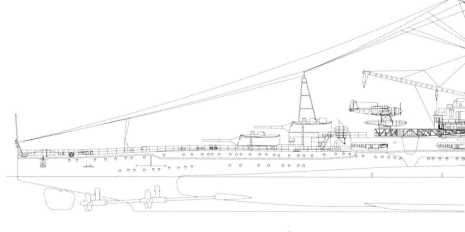

Myoko 1941
Plan & Profile

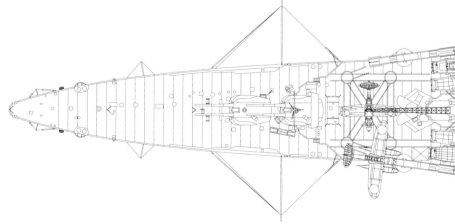

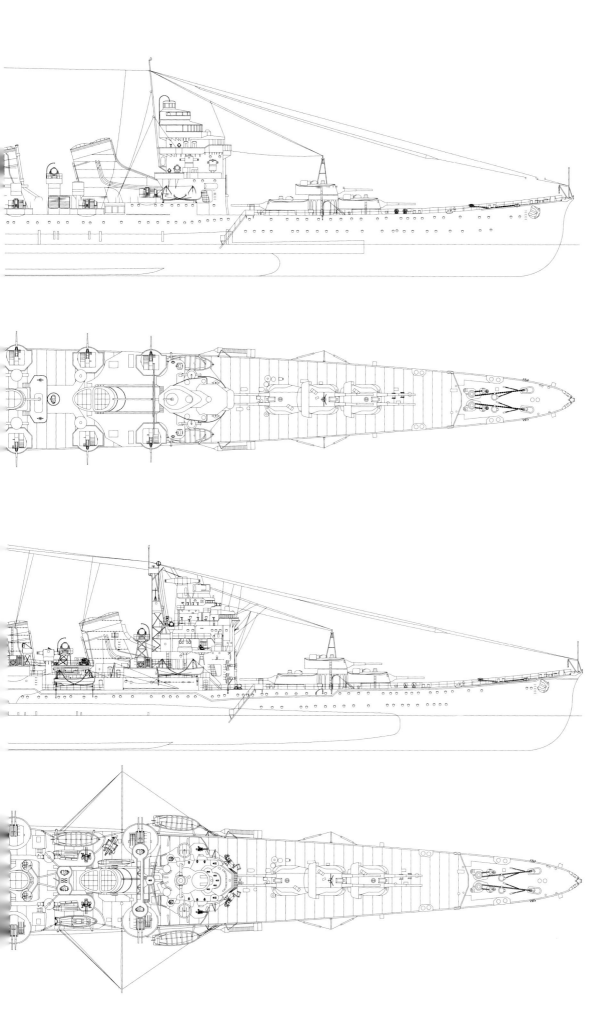

Nachi 1944
Plan & Profile

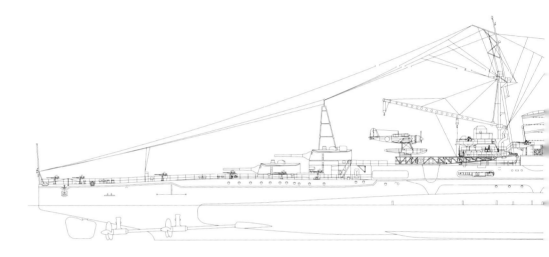

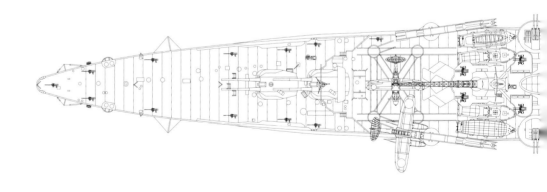

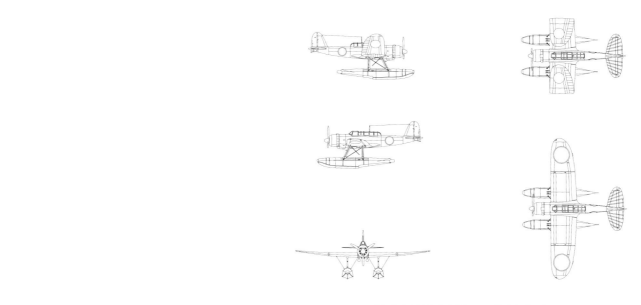

Aichi E13A1 Type 0 'Jake'

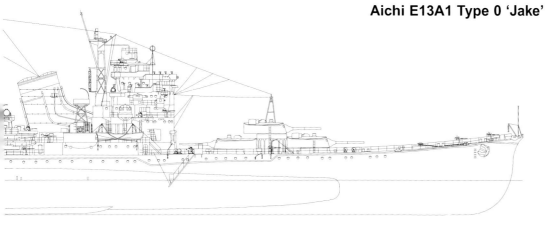

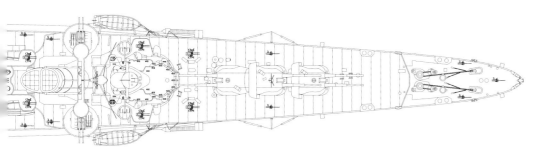

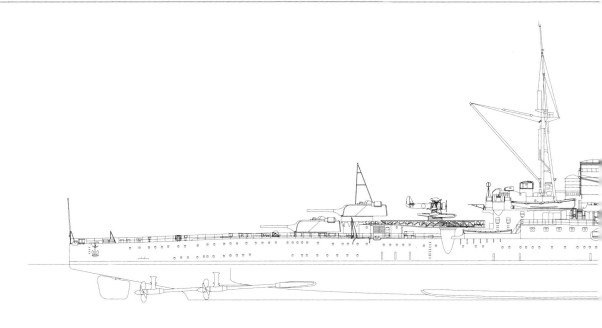

Takao 1932
Plan & Profile

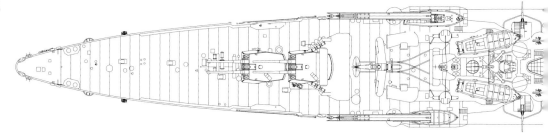

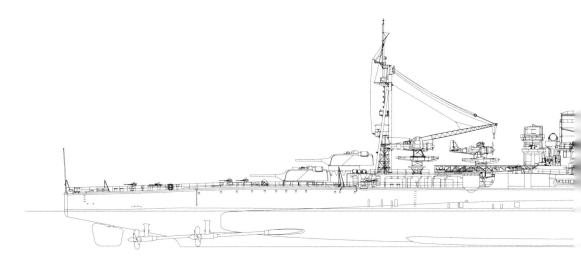

Takao 1944
Plan & Profile

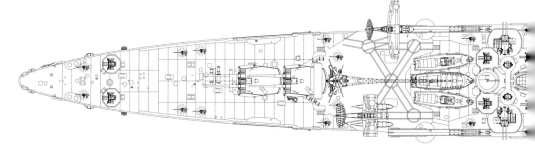

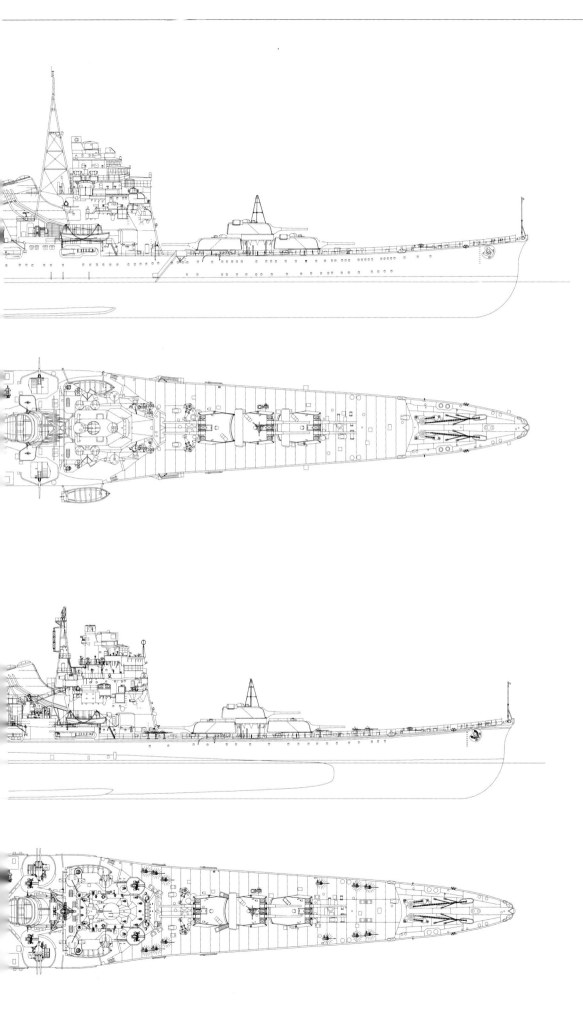

Aircraft Deployed					
Aircraft (Allied codename) service dates	Max speed km/h	Cruising	Range km	Power Plant	Armament
E2N1	172	120	600	300hp Mitsubishi	One 7.7mm MG
E1Y3	189	139	1,156	450hp Lorraine	1 x 7.7mm, 1 x 220kg bomb
E4N2 Type 90-2 Dec 1932 to Dec 1936	232			460hp Jupiter	2 x 7.7mm, 2 x 30kg bombs
E7K2 Type 94 ('Alf') Aug 1939 to Fall 1942	256	160	1,900	870hp Zuisei 11	3 x 7.7mm, 1 x 120kg bomb
E8N2 Type 95 ('Dave') Dec 1936 to Fall 1942	300	185	890	580hp Kotobuki	2 x 7.7mm, 2 x 60kg bombs
E13Al Type 0 ('Jake') Fall 1942 to 1945	375	220	2090	1,020hp Kinsei 43	1 x 20mm, 1 x 7.7mm, 1 x 250kg bomb
F1M2 Type 0 ('Pete') Fall 1942 to 1945	375	200	740	875hp Zusei 13	3 x 7.7mm, 1 x 120kg bomb

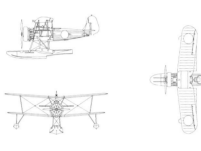

Nakajima E4N2 Type 90-2

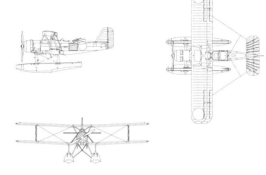
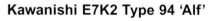

Kawanishi E7K2 Type 94 'Alf'

This is the Nakajima E8N2 Type 94 'Dave' two-seat reconnaissance floatplane on *Ashigara* in 1937 or 1938. The class used two-seat aircraft for tactical reconnaissance and shell-splash spotting. One was carried on the port catapult, as shown here. The starboard catapult carried a longer-range three-seat floatplane used for tactical reconnaissance. In this time period that would be the E7K1 Type 94 'Alf'.

As designed the *Takao* class had a small hangar just aft of the mainmast. This photograph of *Takao* taken between 1936 and 1937 looks forward into the hangar and at the mainmast. After her modernisation this area was enclosed by a shelter deck and the mainmast was moved to approximately the point where this photograph was taken.

Left: The E13AI Type 0 'Jake' three-seat reconnaissance floatplane came into service late in 1942, replacing the E7K2 Type 94 'Alf'. With a range of 2,090km she was used for long range reconnaissance. This photograph from May 1943 shows a 'Jake' being catapulted from the *Ashigara* in the Java Sea.

Below: Another photograph of *Takao* on 21 December 1939 after Modernisation shows the well within the extended shelter deck. This well was just forward of the aircraft deck and contained the ship's boats. The cradles for these boats are shown in the photograph. An E7K2 Type 94 'Alf', three-seat long-range reconnaissance floatplane is shown at centre. The E7K2 replaced the E7K1 'Alf' in August 1939. The wings for two E8N2 Type 95 'Dave', two-seat tactical reconnaissance aircraft are shown flanking the 'Alf'. The 'Dave' was the standard two-seat cruiser floatplane from December 1936 to fall 1942.

Below: The aircraft deck was one area reworked in the Modernisation of *Takao* and *Atago*. This photograph shows *Takao* after her 1939 Modernisation, with the aircraft deck now one level higher atop an enclosed shelter deck that was extended to No 4 barbette. The mainmast has also been relocated to just in front of No 4 barbette. Shown are a E8N2 Type 95 'Dave' tactical reconnaissance aircraft on the starboard catapult, which was normally reserved for the three-seat long range reconnaissance floatplane. That aircraft is the E7K2 Type 94 'Alf', which apparently on this occasion is on a spotting trolley on the aircraft deck rail system.

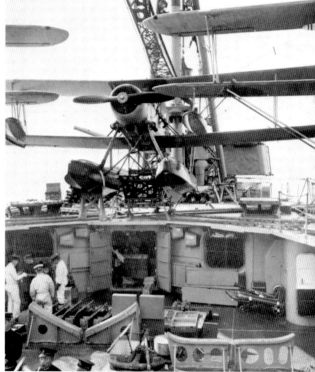

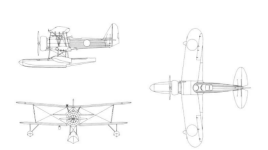

Nahajima E8N1 Type 95 'Dave'

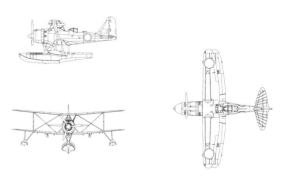

Mitsubishi F1M2 Type 0 'Pete'

BOOKS

Brzezinski, Slawomir, *Chokai, Profile Morskie No 7,* Firma Wydawniczo-Handlowa (Warsaw 1997). Polish Text, 17 pages of line drawing plans, scale not noted, 34 pages.

Brzezinski, Slawomir and **Kopacz, Michal,** *Japanese Cruiser Type Myoko, Fleets of the 20th Century,* Firma Wydawniczo-Handlowa, (Warsaw 2002). Polish Text, text and photos, some line drawings; very limited value for modeller, 58 pages.

Brzezinski, Slawomir and **Nowak, Grzegorz,** *Maya, Profile Morskie No 15,* Firma Wydawniczo-Handlowa, (Warsaw 1999). Polish Text, 23 pages of line drawing plans 1:700 scale and larger of *Maya* 1944, 50 pages.

Brzezinski, Slawomir, *Nachi, Profile Morskie No 61,* Firma Wydawniczo-Handlowa, (Warsaw 2004). Polish-English photograph captions; includes 1:400 scale plans of *Nachi* in 1944, plus colour plan and profile; fittings details in 1:50 to 1:200 scales, 34 pages plus plan inserts.

Bukala, Grzegorz, *Japonskie Krazowniki Ciezkie Typu 'Myoko', Warships of the World No 14,* Wydawca (Warsaw 2002). Polish text, 80 pages, Separate 1:400 scale plans and profiles on *Haguro* 1930, *Ashigara* 1937, *Myoko* 1942, *Nachi* 1944, *Myoko* 1945.

Cutler, Thomas J., *The Battle of Leyte Gulf,* Harper Collins (London 1994).

Dull, Paul, *A Battle History of the Imperial Japanese Navy,* Naval Institute Press (Annapolis, MD 1978).

Hammel, Eric, *Guadalcanal Decision at Sea,* Pacifica Press (Pacifica, CA 1988).

Hoyt, Edwin, *The Lonely Ships, The Life and Death of the U.S. Asiatic Fleet,* David McKay Company (New York 1976).

Lacroix, Eric and **Wells, Linton II,** *Japanese Cruisers of the Pacific War,* Naval Institute Press (Annapolis, MD 1997). This massive 882-page reference covers the design, modification and operations of every class of Japanese cruiser during World War Two and is the best English language reference on the subject.

Launer, Jay, *The Enemies' Fighting Ships,* Sheridan House (New York 1944). Interesting volume for its war-time assessment of the classes but of no value for modelling the ships.

Lorelli, John, *The Battle of the Komandorski Islands,* Naval Institute Press (Annapolis, MD 1984).

Loxton, Bruce, *The Shame of Savo,* Naval Institute Press (Annapolis, MD 1994).

Marder, Arthur, Jacobsen, Mark and **Horsfield, John,** *Old Friends New Enemies, Volume II: The Pacific War 1942-1945,* Oxford University Press (Oxford 1990).

Morison, Samuel Eliot, *History of United States Naval Operations in World War II,* various volumes, Little, Brown and Company (Boston, MA 1984; first published 1948).

Newcomb, Richard, *Savo, The Incredible Naval Debacle off Guadalcanal,* Holt, Rinehart and Winston (New York 1961).

Okamoto, Kouji, *The Heavy Cruiser Takao 1927-1937, Super Illustration,* Model Art Co. Japanese text, overall plans and profiles in 1:500 scale of 1932 and 1935 fits, detail drawings in larger scales, 118 pages almost all of which are line drawings.

Skulski, Janusz, *The Heavy Cruiser Takao, Anatomy of the Ship,* Naval Institute Press (Annapolis, MD 1994). Text in English, text and photographs 39 pages, detailed line drawings 212 pages, 256 pages. Best single source for the modeller of this ship.

Thomas, David, *The Battle of the Java Sea,* Stein and Day (New York 1968).

Warner, Denis and **Peggy,** *Disaster in the Pacific, New Light on the Battle of Savo Island,* Naval Institute Press (Annapolis, MD 1992).

Whitley, M.J., *Cruisers of World War Two An International Encyclopedia,* Brockhampton Press (London 1999). Text in English; good overall survey of all classes of cruiser that served during World War Two.

Wiper, Steve, *Warship Pictorial No 17, IJN Myoko Class Cruisers,* Classic Warships Publishing (Tucson 2002). English Text, Large, clear photographs and colour plan and profile, 74 pages.

JAPANESE MONOGRAPHS AND MAGAZINES

Drawings of Imperial Japanese Naval Vessels Vol 2. Model art volume of line drawings, 94 pages, 12 pages of line drawings on these two classes.

Gakken No 16, The Heavy Cruisers of Takao Class. Text in Japanese, photographs, plans and photographs of 1:100 scale models, 190 pages.

Gakken No 27, The Heavy Cruiser Nachi. Text in Japanese, photographs, plans and photographs of 1:200 scale model, 192 pages.

Japanese Cruisers, Grand Prix 1993. Text in Japanese. This volume of 307 pages contains a treasure trove of detailed line drawings of the fittings and equipment of the Japanese cruisers of World War Two.

Maru Special No 48: Japanese Naval Vessels, 1981. Japanese text. This volume contains 68 pages of interesting photographs and line drawings of the *Takao* and *Atago.*

Maru Special: Mechanisms of Japanese Heavy Cruisers. Japanese text, This is a special, greatly expanded version of the Maru Special publications that compiled very detailed drawings, along with photographs on all six classes of Japanese heavy cruisers. This was apparently the first version of the following listed reference:

Mechanisms of Japanese Warships, Heavy Cruisers, 1991. Japanese text, detailed coverage of fittings in line drawings and photographs, Available in two versions – large format hardback and small size softback.

Random Japanese Warship Details No 1, Tamiya News Supplement. Japanese text. An assortment of line drawings of fittings. 40 pages.

Random Japanese Warship Details No 2, Tamiya News Supplement. Japanese text. An assortment of line drawings of fittings. 41 pages.

Warships of the Imperial Japanese Navy No 8, Myoko and Ashigara, 1997. Text in Japanese, heavy in unusual photographs, 145 pages.

Warships of the Imperial Japanese Navy No 9, Nachi and Haguro, 1997. Text in Japanese, heavy in unusual photographs, 112 pages.

Warships of the Imperial Japanese Navy No 10, Takao Class Heavy Cruisers, 1997. Text in Japanese, heavy in unusual photographs, 136 pages.

Warships of the World, Ships of the Imperial Japanese Navy, 1995. Text in Japanese, large size, clear photographs, 416 pages

PLANS

Miyukikai (Myco) produces 1:200 scale plans of the following cruisers:
MY071 – *Maya* 1944
MY078 – *Takao* 1945
MY092 – *Myoko* 1945
MY100 – *Chokai* 1938
MY101 – *Atago* 1942
MY122 – *Haguro* 1941
MY123 – *Haguro* 1945
MY125 – *Ashigara* 1942

WEBSITES OF CONTRIBUTORS

Gold Medal Models – www.goldmm.com/
Neptun/Navis Models – www.navis-neptun.de/
Pacific Front Hobbies – www.pacificfront.com/
Tom's Modelworks – www.tomsmodelworks.com/
Trident Hobbies – www.tridenthobbies.com/
Voyager Model – www.voyagermodel.com/
White Ensign Models – www.whiteensignmodels.com.

OTHER WEBSITES OF INTEREST

www.combinedfleet.com/kaigun.htm
www.h5.dion.ne.jp/~g-fleet/
www.modelwarships.com/
www2.odn.ne.jp/miyukikai/newpage6.htm
steelnavy.com/